Two Men
who saved France

Two Men
who saved France

PÉTAIN and DE GAULLE

by Major-General Sir Edward Spears

STEIN AND DAY/*Publishers*/New York

Stein and Day / Publishers

7 East 48th Street, New York, N.Y. 10017

Contents

I

II

Map

General Pétain in 1917

Preface

"A crisis of morale in the French nation at war" is a translation of General Pétain's own account of the mutinies in the French Army in 1917, and how, as Commander-in-Chief, he dealt with them.

He gave this to me, asking me to publish it. I have explained in this book why, for so many years, I did not comply with his request. I am glad to do so now, and to make this historic document available, not only to those who have not forgotten Pétain's achievements in the first world war, but also to those who remember him only as the old Marshal who was tried and comdemned by his own countrymen for the part he played in the second.

Pétain and The French Mutinies

The crisis due to the mutinies of the French armies in the spring and early summer of 1917 brought the Allied cause to within nodding distance of defeat, and could have resulted in millions of lives having been sacrificed in vain.

The main credit for their suppression, and therefore for saving France, goes to General Pétain, who had been appointed commander-in-chief in May.

He himself had no doubt as to the gravity of the crisis. Monsieur Painlevé, the Minister of War during this period, writes in his book,[1] "General Pétain told me later that in the days of February and March 1916 at Verdun he had known many anxious hours, but that none had equalled those when he felt the weapon France had entrusted him with would bend and flex in his hands", and Painlevé adds, "No situation ever required more strong and tactful handling. Any weakness would have brought about the dissolution of the army, any brutality its revolt".

And General Franchet d'Esperey, who was Pétain's immensely strong and energetic assistant in dealing with the mutinies, told me then and repeated later that the period when they were occurring was the only time he had felt very serious anxieties during the whole war.

I had never heard of Pétain until the battle of Guise, fought during the great retreat before the battle of the Marne in 1914. At that engagement, Franchet d'Esperey, commanding I Corps, ordered his whole staff to mount, and with flags unfurled and bands playing, placed himself at the head of one of his brigades and led his troops in a successful attack on the German Guards.[2] He exuded energy and confidence and looked the very embodiment of all the martial qualities history and legend attribute to a French general. As he rode by, he spotted a sad, stern-faced officer

[1] *Comment j'ai nommé Foch et Pétain.*
[2] John Terraine, *Western Front*, p. 130.

11

with a drooping moustache the colour of pepper and salt, standing with the small staff of the brigade he had just been promoted to command, watching the amazing spectacle General Franchet d'Esperey provided.

The mounted general had known the brigadier, who was much his senior (Pétain was then 58 years old), when the latter was a lecturer at the Staff College, the *École de Guerre*, and called out to him as he rode by, "What do you think of this manoeuvre, Monsieur le Professeur à l'École de Guerre?"

I was told during the Marne fighting that Pétain, considered a competent but undistinguished officer, had been on the point of being retired, but that at the time of the great German onslaught known as the battle of Charleroi his regiment (the 33rd Infantry) had behaved very well and its commander's imperturbable attitude had been reflected in low losses. At a time when General Joffre, the commander-in-chief, was mercilessly weeding out incompetent commanders, this modest performance, in fact that of not having failed, provided a sufficient reason for Pétain's being entrusted with a brigade.

I got to know Pétain well when he commanded XXXIII Corps on the deadly Lorette Ridge, today covered by a forest of wooden crosses. In those early days of the war it buttressed the Vimy Ridge near the junction with the British army, where my duties as liaison officer with the French often led me. From almost daily visits to this sector, careful examination of the tactical methods employed by Pétain, his use of fire power, the combination of artillery and infantry power, his disciplinary practices which were both firm and stern, the ingenuity with which he set up small factories and workshops to provide him with some of the weapons and objects his men needed but could not obtain from army sources, I soon realised that there was much to be learned from him which could be of benefit to our own army.

Above all, his tactics, which were generally so successful, often led me to question him or to ask permission to be enlightened either by members of his staff or subordinate commanders. Presently he told me that whenever I was near his headquarters at meal times my place would always be laid at his mess, his *'popote'* as the French call it, and I often took advantage of his hospitality. I was very young then, they said I was gay, and the general seemed interested in the fact that I wandered about his line so assiduously, and entertained by the stories of his own men I brought back. He was, I know, enormously amused at an anecdote I told him one day. A remarkable feature of the fighting at the time was that although the British army might be holding the front a couple of miles away, the French army so far as the troops were concerned was almost always completely ignorant of the fact. Our uniforms were also unknown to them, which could, and indeed did, lead on occasion to very awkward situations. In consequence, I, a proud and recent member of the Legion of Honour, had devised a neat method whereby in the British lines only the top of the ribbon appeared above the breast pocket, the medal having dropped into the pocket through a slit in its top, while in the French lines it hung free in all the glory of its red ribbon. The French could be relied on to recognise their own national decoration, I thought, and generally they did. On this occasion, however, near where the communication trenches emerged into the open, I met a French patrol who did not attempt to salute. Well . . . I shrugged, but having gone some little distance I heard the patrol leader call, "Hey there, you Boche, stop!" This was too much. They had mistaken my red cap band for the German one. I turned back in great indignation, asking why, if they could not tell a British uniform when they saw one, they could not at least recognise the Legion of Honour. The corporal looked taken aback for a moment, then an expression of cunning spread over his face and he said, with a strong Midi accent: "Sure we saw you were wearing the Legion of Honour but we thought you might have been given it for surrendering!"

I presently found out, and wondered at my discovery, that General Pétain had a marked sense of humour deeply concealed under his frozen exterior, like *edelweiss* beneath a snowdrift, as unexpected as a spring of fresh water in the desert. It was sometimes expressed in stories of the Midi, drawn from the distant days when he had been a *Chasseur Alpin* and had served both in the mountains and in the exuberant towns of Provence.

I remember, for instance, his telling me that playing up to the Marseillais' inordinate pride in the city's main street, the Cannebière—which its citizens never doubted was a frequent subject of conversation by the great ones of this world nor that the President of the Republic would often say to his prime minister, "What do you think they are saying on the Cannebière today?" —he would go up to a peaceful bourgeois taking the air on the famous thoroughfare and with an air of the utmost innocence ask him if he would be so kind as to tell him the name of the street they were in. It seems that invariably this question, displaying such an insulting ignorance of one of the world's best known streets, would cause the Marseillais in question to become speechless with rage. Hitting the pavement with his stick, he would shout: "And this, what do you take it for – *prenez vous ça pour de la m. —?*"

As I got to know Pétain better, I became used to his very frank criticism of things and people, so I was not surprised when I heard that later, when he was in command of the Verdun sector, he had expressed some very pessimistic views to the President of the Republic who was visiting his HQ. When Monsieur Poincaré asked him the reason for his lack of optimism, he said, "What can you expect, *Monsieur le Président*, when we are neither commanded nor governed", which, when you remember that in France the President presides at meetings of the government, was saying quite a lot.

I only saw General Pétain occasionally during the period which followed the German withdrawal to the Hindenburg line in 1917, but I sometimes visited him and the other army group commanders whom I knew well, hoping to find out what effect they really thought this enemy master-stroke would have on the offensive which General Nivelle persisted in carrying out with but few modifications to meet fundamentally changed circumstances.

It was certain they must have many reservations, and although I did not expect them to criticise the commander-in-chief, I thought I could gather some impression of their views, and I did. They were all doubtful concerning the prospects of the forth-coming attack. General Nivelle, however, was meeting every doubt voiced by anyone, including members of the government, with unassailable optimism, proclaiming that the speed, weight and violence of the onslaught would carry all before it.

After these occasional meetings with Pétain in the early months of 1917, I did not see him again until May.

Appointed on the 5th May, 1917, head of the newly created British Military Mission to the French government, I soon learnt that after the appalling failure of the Nivelle offensive the govern-ment was hesitating between appointing Foch or Pétain to the supreme command in succession to Nivelle.

One of the factors in favour of Foch in their eyes was that he was supposed to enjoy the complete confidence and reverent admiration of the British, a somewhat distorted view, for which General Wilson, now chief liaison officer at French GQG, was in the main responsible.

I could only pray that the choice of the government would fall on Pétain.

Since the autumn of 1914 I had had many opportunities of ob-serving General Foch at close but respectful distances, across the disciplined miles reckoned in stars and gold braid, the heaps of medals that separate a young captain from an old and famous general. I had heard him at conferences, listened to him expound-ing his views and giving his orders. I had had meals with him and followed him on visits to the front. In fact I had had opportunities of measuring his great height against my inches, and the impres-sion left, not an unfriendly one, was mild astonishment that so re-nowned a warrior in fact produced successes that were so un-earth shaking and how small were the mice this mountain gave birth to. My personal observation of him as a commander so far was that he had immense moral courage, but that his reserves were invariably badly placed.

As between these considerable commanders I thought, judging from the viewpoint of my unimpressive status but by now considerable experience, that General Pétain would be a far more satis-factory commander-in-chief. It was reasonable also to hope that the French army would, under Pétain, carry out the offensives in support of our own to which they were pledged, and that the harm done by the Calais Conference, at which Lloyd George had placed the British army under Nivelle's command, would be undone.

At the end of April, General Pétain, at the suggestion of Mon-sieur Painlevé, always an admirer of things British, was appointed Chief of the General Staff with powers analogous to those of Sir William Robertson, Chief of the Imperial General Staff, until such time as he became commander-in-chief. General Foch would then succeed him as Chief of Staff.

The appointments of Pétain as Commander-in-Chief and Foch as Chief of the General Staff were decided on by the government on the 15th May and published in the *Journal Officiel* the next day.

I learnt the great news from General Pétain himself within a few minutes of his having been informed of it by Monsieur Pain-levé, at the Ministry for War, rue St Dominique. This was hardly five minutes away from the Conseil Supérieur de la Guerre, Boulevard des Invalides, where Pétain had his office, on the ground floor, I remember, not very far from the entrance. My own office was on the floor just above his.

Had I felt any elation and pride at being almost the first to hear of his appointment from the new commander-in-chief himself, it was of short duration. Pétain was anxious to reach his headquarters as quickly as possible and wished to entrust me with a message before he left. "I am going to Compiègne (French GHQ) to take over command in a few minutes," he said. "By the time I get there General Wilson [the chief British liaison officer] must have left. *C'est un intriguant.*" (He is an intriguer.)

There was no question of not doing what I was told, but it was very much the equivalent of being ordered to deliver your own professional death warrant, for I knew this vindictive man would never forgive the bearer of such bad tidings, and I feared that his influence with Foch might tend to negate the good will I believed I had been able to acquire with the French army over the years.

Compiègne is only fifty miles from Paris and even in that war of execrable roads it was not a long journey, so in order to carry out Pétain's orders in the time available I dashed upstairs to telephone to my chief, General Maurice[1] at the War Office. I do not know how he arranged things, but General Wilson had disappeared from the GQG when Pétain arrived.

It was on the same day, the 15th May, as I was being driven to the Ministry of the Interior on the far side of the Champs Elysées, that my car was stopped near the Rond Point des Champs Elysées by a procession of girls carrying banners.

These were the junior employees of the great 'couture' houses, some of whom had their establishments in the neighbourhood, girls called technically and pathetically 'les petites mains', the small hands, and indeed most of the demonstrators were very young. They were some of the vast number of girls employed by the grande couture, the fashion houses, who, because they emerged into the streets for lunch at noon, midi, were called charmingly 'les midinettes'. The crowd were evidently sympathetic and rather amused and touched by the unusual sight of women being so bold as to demonstrate in the public streets.

When I learnt subsequently that the strike was for an increase of one sou, five centimes, a halfpenny an hour, I felt very moved by these young things whose demands were so modest and who doubtless worked very hard for their small pittance. I followed the procession for some time, hoping to learn something of public opinion by observing the reactions of the passers-by. These included many soldiers on leave, and it was noticeable that their reaction was different from that of the civilians. They showed anger, a desire to identify themselves with the girls' protest, and many stepped off the pavement to join them, often taking their arms, which tended to give the whole thing the aspect of a jolly party. But I remembered the expressions of the soldier sympathisers and

[1] Director of Military Operations.

compared the impression they gave me with an incident which
had occurred a few days earlier in a more populous part of Paris
when, sitting in the smart French car of a friend, there had been a
slight accident, and the attitude of a typical French crowd had
been anything but friendly at the sight of a foreign uniform. A
sergent de ville had intervened, a member of the excellent Paris
police force, and all had been well, but the obvious, close-to-
the-surface, easily aroused hostility of men on leave against possible '*embusqués*' was striking.

I learnt from this incident also that these same '*embusqués*',
whom I believed I could identify, sleek men in uniform, very
different from the '*poilus*' among whom I had lived for so long,
were anxious to seize upon any opportunity to demonstrate a
bellicosity their mien belied. This was also the first occasion when
I realised the very deep and natural resentment of the Parisians
against foreign soldiers who, strikingly different from their own,
gave the anxious civilians the impression that their capital was
being invaded by foreign play-boys aping soldiers, while their
men, from lads to ancient territorials, fed the insatiable holocaust
of the war.

It had never dawned on me to doubt the steadfast resolution of
the French nation, any more than the thought would have
occurred to me that the army would not hold out until the resources of America had built up those of the Alliance into an
overwhelmingly irresistible force. Nor do I believe that either
the French army or the French people ever doubted each other,
though some high-ranking and responsible commanders and
staff officers distrusted the loyalty of a few politicians and in
consequence felt some qualms concerning the morale of those
sections of the industrial population which were subject to influence from the Left and the extreme Left.

The worst pessimists, until despair at the bloody failure of the
spring offensives affected the army, were to be found among
those who ran no danger, civilians far from the front.

In May 1917, all I knew of French politics and of the situation
in the interior of the country I had gleaned from the officers I

worked with, some of whom were Deputies. I knew there were some trouble makers, some pacifists, some industrial centres which gave the staffs concern, and some very dangerous elements, probably in German pay, who tried to subvert men on leave, to spread pessimism through the post, and by every means to spread the doctrines of the Russian revolution, of which the two Russian brigades in France were the focal point. I was also aware from the blank spaces in the papers that there were those anxious to print views the military authorities did not approve of. I knew that Monsieur Malvy, the Minister of the Interior, was the bogey of the general staffs, inexplicably tolerated by the government in spite of his disreputable associates and more than doubtful friends. This indulgence was assumed by the army to be due to his influence with the trade unions whose political support he enjoyed.[1]

During my early days in Paris everything was strange.

The officers I had to deal with at the Ministry of War and at the Conseil Supérieur de la Guerre were always friendly, but complete confidence can only come with time, and it presently became evident that I should have to define the scope of my own mission, and what were my attributions. Knowledge of political trends was all-important to the military authorities, but how far could I go without trespassing on the Embassy's preserves? The Field Army I had henceforth nothing to do with, that was the responsibility of our military missions with the GQG, the French General Headquarters, yet the relations of the French government with its own army were very much my business. I also presently realised that, very quietly in the background, sustained by officers on leave, there existed in Paris a discreet and very pleasant life, just what the fighting army resented but was only too glad to participate in when opportunity offered. I did not know to what extent events in the interior of France concerned me, or whether this also was a diplomatic preserve through the Consuls General. Presently my work evolved to cover the whole immense field of France at war, but meanwhile the apprehensions I voiced to the

[1] Clemenceau when he became prime minister later tried him for his life. He got off with five years' exile.

new set of French officers and officials I now worked with concerning the morale of the country, the reaction of the provinces to the appalling setbacks and blood-lettings of Nivelle's offensive, were met by reassuring but vague generalities. And I was not unduly alarmed at the situation; with Pétain as commander-in-chief and Painlevé as Minister of War everything is bound to turn out right I thought. Painlevé I saw practically every day. His integrity was impressive, but I never fathomed the extreme depths of his radical convictions which, for instance, led him to believe that Sarrail was a good general because he was a man of the extreme Left. He liked and admired the British and had a great regard for Mr Lloyd George. I got on well with him, though it took some time to establish a friendship that once cemented lasted as long as his life.

I sometimes wondered whether M. Painlevé had not wandered into politics by mistake. It was of absorbing interest to watch this mathematician set his precise brain to solve the imponderable problems raised by the military situation, attempting to find logical answers to moral questions, to state in absolute quantities such things as fear, lost hopes, the desperate longing for rest and home. It was an education in itself to observe him assess and attempt to adjust the point of view of the Ministry of War staff, of the GQG, of the Cabinet and of the Chamber and Senate. And he managed it somehow because he was so honest.

It was when working with him that I learnt something of the interplay of allies on each other, each with their national problems to be adjusted to those of the others, and the endless examination of the enemy's situation, and what were his resources and consequently his plans. There was also the immensely depressing task of fathoming the putrescent depths the Russian army had fallen into, and a new problem which loomed ever more disquietingly: the determination of General Pershing to hold back the slowly growing American army until it could fight as a fully constituted force, whereas the Allied forces were withering for lack of men. Pershing refused to provide men until he could do so in divisions and army corps.

I knew nothing of the mutinies until, on the morning of the 4th June, I met General de Maud'huy outside the entrance to the *Conseil Supérieur de la Guerre*. In spite of the difference in age and rank between us I could claim him as a very old friend. In fact I revered and loved him. He was so rich in kindness and genuine chivalry, so understanding of the feelings of simple private soldiers, so exuberantly brave, that he enriched every soul he ever came in contact with. I had met him during the battle of the Marne at a moment when unpleasantly large shells were falling, causing even him to incline his head as one does to keep one's hat on in a high wind.

"How do you like the war?" he had shouted through the noise. "I have not had a single dunning letter since it started," I shouted back, "which is a nice change." This must have appealed to him, for he often referred to the young English cavalry officer who, before Montmirail, developed the thesis that there was something to be said for battles since tailors and their bills were allergic to them.

When he commanded the 10th Army in Artois I was a frequent guest at his table, merely warning in when attending. He was not a great commander and had lost the command of his army, but his courage and magnetism made him an unequalled leader of men in war. After a period of unemployment during which he had begged for any post that entailed fighting, an infantry company would do, he had been given the command of the XII Corps.

Delighted as always to see him, I asked him on that 4th June what he was doing in Paris. Although used to being treated by him with complete frankness, I was very much taken aback and greatly concerned to be told that his corps was engaged in dealing with widespread disorders on the Aisne front. He had had to take charge of two of the regiments (six battalions) in which trouble had occurred.

He took me for a walk along the Boulevard des Invalides and gave me many details of what had happened. "The trouble, which looked uncommonly like a mutiny, broke out all at once and bore every sign of having been very carefully organised, apparently by socialist leaders from the interior." Officers' servants had been kept in the dark and the officers had no idea of what was going to happen. In the units he had had to deal with so far the men's attitude was extremely correct. They formulated their complaints to their officers and were at pains to explain that they were fond of them and wanted to keep them. The main burden of their grievances was that they were sick of the war and demanded peace. They also suffered from a deep sense of injustice. They all knew there were thousands of 'embusqués' in the interior, men drawing big money in soft and safe jobs, courting the women of men who were fighting. For the hardest grievance of all to bear was the endless disappointment over leave, and the unfair way in which it was granted, without rhyme or reason, units longest in line often being given the lowest priority.

The general said that in his view the profound reason for an outbreak that had occurred with such spontaneousness could only be that the troops had all had a practically identical reaction to the failure of the April offensive. "*A quoi bon?*" "What's the good?" and he indicated clearly that somehow the new commander-in-chief must infuse a new hope into the army and that this could only be done by success. "But first discipline must be re-established." If this was the view of one who understood the soldiers so well and had such sympathy for their point of view although a strict disciplinarian, then it must be so, I thought. "The men have great faith in Pétain," he said, "but there have been so many changes in the command of corps and divisions that there are at present no general officers at that level who have personal influence on the mutinous regiments."

He referred to the depressing effect on morale of some very pessimistic articles by influential deputies which were appearing in the daily press.

A curious aspect of the trouble in the affected regiments was that the machine-gun detachments generally kept out of it and in some cases set up their guns in battery under their officers against the remainder of the regiment. Pioneer sections tended to do the same, from which it might be concluded that detachments working in close touch with an officer they knew well had a point of view of their own which prevented their being carried away by the wave of general indiscipline.

General de Maud'huy was relying on the cavalry regiments to round up mutinous units and to represent disciplined authority generally, but he hinted broadly, and his very mobile features made it clear, that the men hated the job and had made it obvious that it was most unlikely that they could be induced to answer a similar call again.

Then he spoke of the influence of the news from Russia on the troops.

This was disastrous and provided the ideal fulcrum for the 'mauvaises têtes' in the regiments and the defeatists in the interior, and a theme song for all the elements of the Left, the soft underbelly of the nation. News of the Russian army fascinated the soldiers.

The papers said that in the Russian army officers were no longer saluted. This appealed as a grand idea. Saluting was a silly formality anyhow. There were also reports that in Russia officers now took part in fatigues. Some thought this a splendid notion but others thought it was going too far. The election of officers found general favour. Who better than the men knew the good officers?

It seemed as if in some obscure way the men felt that the spirit of their own revolution was sweeping over Russia, but there was one great difference that today's mutineers had not perceived: the men of the 1790's had insisted on being led to war to throw the enemy out of France, whereas the present-day admirers of Russia held a contrary point of view. The mutineers were also totally unaware that the tattered but freedom-loving soldiers of the Revolution who had swept across Europe in countless victories had been quite useless until very strict discipline had been re-established and the election of officers abolished.

De Maud'huy said that one of the dreadful aspects of the present crisis was that it was often the very best regiments, those that had been ungrudging in their efforts, exemplary in their staunchness, that were giving most trouble.

He concluded by telling me that there had been symptoms of similar trouble in the army at the time the two years Military Service Bill had been introduced. Care had then been taken to keep away staff officers, gendarmes and generals from the regiments whose discipline had been affected.

As he left me the general said he believed the trouble would be over in five or six days.

He was over-optimistic.

I reported all this on the same day in a letter to General Maurice, Director of Military Operations at the War Office, through whom I reported to the CIGS, adding that I gathered that the only measures being taken at the moment were to separate disaffected units from the remainder of the troops and send them off in different directions.

Meanwhile the War Cabinet in London and Sir William Robertson, the CIGS, although completely unaware of these facts, were uneasy, sensing something of the low morale of the French army as a result of the military failures of April. Robertson wrote to Sir Douglas Haig on the 12th May that the unsettled state of affairs in France together with the probability of a separate peace by Russia might have a detrimental effect on the efficient prosecution of the offensive operations agreed between the two governments.

To this Sir Douglas replied on the 18th that he maintained the view previously expressed that action of a wearing-down kind must be maintained.

But meanwhile the War Office had expressed further concern in a letter to Sir Douglas dated the 16th May.

Their fears were aroused because the printed French versions of the agreements reached between the two governments concerning future plans made no reference to the promise given by the French government to continue offensive action. The CIGS thought this might mean that the French government had, on reflection, decided not to bind itself to carry out its undertaking. He went on to say, expressing the views of the War Cabinet, that a situation was not to be allowed to develop in which "costly operations were embarked upon in which the British Army was left to fight practically alone".

Whereupon, intent upon clarifying the situation, Sir Douglas arranged a meeting with General Pétain on the 18th May at Amiens, three days after the latter had assumed command of the French armies. Haig was impressed with Pétain's frank and straightforward manner.

He struck him as clear-headed and businesslike, and he was outspoken concerning the unrest within the French army.

The English commander asked the French general about his offensive plans and was told that he had four attacks in preparation. The first one was at Malmaison and was scheduled to take place on the 10th June (it was in fact carried out in October) and another by fifteen divisions at Verdun to be delivered towards the end of July (it took place on the 20th August).

The British Official History states that the British commander said that these operations might be synchronised with the projected British offensives in Flanders, which he described in some detail. General Pétain objected to the distant aims of these operations, pointing out that this was contrary to the advice he had given at the Paris conference, when he had urged that operations during 1917 should have strictly limited objectives. Sir Douglas said that his successive objectives would be so limited. The French general said that what was essential was that the British army should attack. Where and how was Sir Douglas' business.

It may be presumed that General Pétain, like General de Maud'-huy, underestimated the gravity of the trouble in the French army and how deep rooted was the malady born of years of hardship, neglect and disappointment.

Up to the date of the meeting of the two commanders-in-chief the signs of unrest had been disquieting enough, based in the first instance on the exasperated despair of a division ordered back for an attack over ground where it had previously failed, whereas other divisions in the same case were allowed to rest.

From then on further and ever graver acts of insubordination were reported over a widening area.

Thereupon General Pétain, the mutinies having reached their climax, though he could not have known this, very loyally sent his chief of staff, General Debeney, to see Sir Douglas Haig on the 2nd June. The situation must have appeared well nigh catastrophic at the French GQG, but General Pétain lost neither his head nor his confidence either in himself or in his army. But he rightly felt he was in duty bound to inform his British colleague, to some extent at least.

What General Debeney told Sir Douglas no one will ever know, for the Frenchman pledged him to secrecy and the British general treated what he had been told as a military secret and apparently did not tell even the most senior and intimate members of his staff anything at all precise. He certainly did not tell the CIGS, beyond making it clear that it was essential, in view of the exhaustion and discouragement of the French army, that the British offensives should be maintained. It is certainly not impossible that he felt that had the British government had any inkling of the true state of the French army they would have panicked and forbidden the offensive he was about to undertake and which was to prove such a success: that of the Messines ridge.

This, and little more, was known and appreciated by the very senior British commanders and staff officers at GHQ. It was recognised and acknowledged that the French intended only to maintain such offensive action as was open to them in the circumstances, that is, the continuation of the artillery battle on the Aisne and the preparation for the attacks already decided upon, to be launched as soon as possible so as to ensure that the German divisions on the French front were maintained there, and not allowed to slip away to the British sector.

It has always seemed strange to me that at this period, at the height of the mutinies, when there were only two completely reliable divisions between Soissons and Paris,[1] the British Military Mission at French GHQ, under Sir Henry Wilson, which was sixty officers strong, had no inkling that there was anything seriously amiss with the French army. When General de Maud'huy

[1] *Comment j'ai nommé Foch et Pétain*, p. 143.

told me of the situation, it did not occur to me that Sir Douglas
Haig was not fully appraised of it by Sir Henry Wilson. Wilson
was apparently shown the notes made by General Debeney of his
interview with Sir Douglas Haig, but given no information about
the mutinies.

On the day after my talk with General de Maud'huy I wrote to
General Maurice again and on a kindred subject.

That morning, driving past the base of the Eiffel Tower as usual
on my way to my office from my flat, I noticed that the Indo-
Chinese soldiers who usually guarded it had disappeared, replaced
by old Territorials. This evidently meant something, possibly
something serious. I had obtained with some difficulty that my
mission should be composed half of French, half of British
officers, and my second-in-command was French. I asked the
French officers to find out the explanation of this sudden innova-
tion.

By lunch time I knew what had occurred. On the previous
night, in a tumultuous and populous quarter of Paris, at St Ouen,
a row had started in a café between some Annamite and French
soldiers. Women were certainly involved.

The French, soldiers and civilians alike, did not like these
secretive, unsmiling little Asiatics. Furthermore, the people, unable to speak their language, felt completely cut off from these
strangers, whose mysterious presence made them uneasy. Why
were they in Paris anyway? If they had been brought from their
distant land to fight, then the trenches and not Paris was the place
for them. And the deeply suspicious French temperament was not
slow to draw the conclusion that the government intended to use
these yellow men to bend the people to its will. They were
worse than the police or the gendarmes, there was no appeal to
anything recognisably human behind those expressionless masks.
And so the café row degenerated rapidly into a riot. The French of
the class encountered at St Ouen were prone to noise and angry
gestures. The Annamites knew nothing of the French Revolution,

but they doubtless saw for themselves how soon a Paris mob can become murderously dangerous. They fled back to their barracks, no doubt in fear for their lives, the mob in hot pursuit, and closed the doors, which the French began to batter. The Annamites ran for their rifles and opened fire, that is, fired some shots from windows at their pursuers. There were some casualties, I was told (in point of fact one woman was killed and several people wounded). The mob was infuriated and ready for anything.

By this time the authorities had been alerted and the wise decision was taken to get the Annamites out of Paris immediately; they all left on the morning of the 5th.

The bare bones of this I reported to General Maurice that evening (the 5th June) and told him of the excitement the incident had caused in the populous centres of the capital, feelings reflected in Parliament, where it was being proclaimed in the lobbies that coloured troops had been employed against the people. I was able to inform him that M. Painlevé had made a great speech which had carried the House and quiet was restored. The incident would do harm in the country, I warned, for it would be widely spread and certainly exaggerated.

I had asked to see General Weygand in the morning and told him I understood there was trouble in the army. Would he be so kind as to tell me what it amounted to? He said he would be glad to do so, but in the strictest confidence of course.

There had in fact been some trouble, but it was not as serious as it might have been, for the men had no military grievances and were in no way dissatisfied with their military chiefs or with their leadership. But on the other hand they were profoundly discontented with the political direction of the war. The whole trouble emanated from the interior and was hatched out in the unwholesome political atmosphere created by left-wing politicians. The result was that discouraging and even defeatist propaganda reached the troops unchecked in some areas; it even penetrated to rest billeting zones behind some sectors of the front.

The greatest responsibility for the trouble, said General Weygand, rested with the Minister of the Interior, M. Malvy, who was very weak. He was himself quite satisfied that order would soon be restored provided the government was firm. He also thought General Pétain's influence would be very helpful, which was the sort of cool praise I would have expected from that quarter.

Well, I was now at least aware of what it was desired we should believe.

At the 'Cabinet du Ministre', that is, from the officers who worked in very close touch with the Minister of War, preparing and digesting for him the immense amount of information reaching him from the GQG and other sources affecting the army, I gathered a different preoccupation as far as the British were concerned. That they were worried about the morale of the army I could feel and sense, not that I asked many questions. I never did. I always learnt more from my eyes than my ears and the required information seemed to be generally forthcoming in good time. There was an obvious and apologetic anxiety not to let the British down. The problem of the French was clear and was felt to be humiliating.

These officers and the Minister were fully aware of the way the British had been treated during the Nivelle period of command, and in the light of recent events these memories could not evoke satisfaction in the hearts of fair-minded men. It was generally recognised in political as well as in military circles that the British had carried out their part of the bargain with success, and resentment against Nivelle served to underline their quiet reliability under very trying circumstances. In fact eulogy of all things British became an embarrassment, so much so that lately unsolicited praise for British military operations and bravery in action had crept into the French press, which had literally for years, as if by some secret covenant, shrouded the British army in a fog of silence.

Indeed, presently M. Painlevé, in a parliamentary speech, cited British tactics as an example General Pétain was following. After describing the new commander-in-chief's methods he went on: "These were the same which you have seen applied with such

mastery in the last British battles [Messines] whose results you are
aware of and which were obtained at the cost of losses so small
that they seem incredible."

General de Maud'huy's information had posed a personal problem as far as I was concerned. Although, as I have said, it did not
occur to me that our Mission at the GQG had not reported on the
unrest in the army, I also knew that its duties were connected with
staff questions and that it would not have been the habit of any of
its members to visit army units and find out for themselves what
the situation was, nor would it have been proper that they should
have done so. They would have been moving among strangers
and would have found out nothing. Their presence would certainly have been resented as an intrusion. On the other hand, my
work had always been with the fighting units and the staffs of
lower formations, and I was certain that if I were to return to the
divisions whose units I knew I could form a pretty exact picture
of the morale of the troops over a wide front.

I had been doing so for years, giving my chiefs a sympathetic
but true picture of the French units among whom I lived.

As this information, always important, was probably now more
so than it had ever been, ought I not to try to provide it and report
to my chiefs in London?

But it had been clearly laid down that my duties no longer lay
with the army but with the Ministry of War, and I had been the
first to insist that our Mission at the GQG should give up the
rather desultory liaison they had maintained by occasional visits
to Paris and leave me solely responsible for the War Department,
confining themselves exclusively to the offices at Compiègne.
If I myself infringed a rule I had so vehemently upheld, would
not the Mission, which I was so anxious should be a success, fade
away in disharmony and recriminations, killed at its inception by
my fault?

But such considerations did not cause me to hesitate long. The
one thing that really mattered was that my chiefs should have a
true picture of what was going on in the French army. Any other
consideration was of little moment. So, asking no one's leave and

telling no one of my intention, I left Paris early next morning,
the 6th June, at high speed and quite alone save for the chauffeur
and the French soldier who had been my constant escorts since
the retreat from Mons, making for the village of Vic-sur-Aisne,
which had been Franchet d'Esperey's advance HQ when I was
working and living with him not much more than a month ago.
I avoided Compiègne and questions.

The examining posts were notoriously obstructive and would
probably be more so than usual now. However, I was only stopped
two or three times by the usual exasperatingly slow-witted Territorial posts who finally grasped the significance of the special
passes I carried. Generally speaking the quickest way was to spell
them to them.

When approaching Vic-sur-Aisne I was stopped by a rather
nervous lieutenant standing alone. "*Où allez vous?*" "Where are
you going?" he questioned, but before I had time to answer,
suddenly aware of my uniform, asked, "*Êtes-vous anglais?*"
"Are you English?"

Then, "If I were you, *à votre place*, I do not think I would go
down this road; not long since a car came past me, then came back,
the officer in it saying he had been stopped by a post wearing red
rosettes who refused to let him pass unless he went into the village
to be interrogated, goodness knows by whom, so he turned his
car and came back. I myself," he went on, "had come in the
regimental horse cart, sent to find out the position in the village
ahead, but when I heard what the officer in the car said I thought
I had better stop and find out more, but the driver, as soon as I
got out, whipped up his horse and was gone."

Leaving him, I took side roads, trusting that my faithful escort
would vouch for me in case of need, as he had often done before,
and finally reached my destination, which turned out to be as
strange an experience as I have ever had. When I had left it it was
full of movement, soldiers everywhere, sentries much in evidence.
Now it was completely and absolutely deserted, which in itself
was uncanny, for there were normally no empty villages in the
army zone. I tramped about but there was not a soul to be seen.

Now one thing I had been looking forward to on this trip, and that was to see my dog, Rex, the superb police dog trained by the Paris police who had been given me by one of the Balzan brothers. I had left him in charge of Captain Altmeyer (who commanded a corps next to the British in the Second World War). If I could not find anything else I would locate my dog if he was there, so halting at street corners I whistled my loudest, and presently, after an interval which, I knew quite well, was used by Rex in a careful test of oral memory to make sure there was no mistake and it was indeed his master returned, I heard a terrific and joyful howl and knew he was on his hind legs somewhere yelling his head off.

Following up the sound, I soon located and released him, and he galloped about me round the village, but could give me no indication of where the other occupants had gone, so I had to leave him where I had found him, determined that, come what might, he at least should not be forgotten in his barn.

I drove on towards the front, keeping a sharp look-out, and quite soon came on a barrier, a ladder across the road between two carts, and a post of men, their *'capotes'* (the combined coat and jacket of the French soldier) unbuttoned, wearing red rosettes.

An NCO was in charge, polite but inquisitive. "Where are you going? What are you looking for?" "I would like to see your commanding officer." The man looked cross but not threatening. "Not possible, the officers are over there, but for the moment, *pour le moment*, they are seeing no one. But what do you want? You are English? *Vous êtes anglais?*"

"Yes." "*Ah, les anglais*," and he shrugged as if to convey the idea: "Ah, the English and what good are they?" I thought it wise as well as proper to seem aloof, manifesting a shocked surprise, and when I was asked again what I wanted, said that the English army was attacking the Germans further north as was agreed and that I had been sent to see what support we were being given by the French. " 'Attack?' We aren't attacking. *On en a mare.* We are fed up."

"It is worse than last year. The wire was cut nowhere – it was a massacre."

"We can't beat the Boches, so why get killed uselessly? *A quoi bon*? What's the use? The generals don't know the answer," and some more of the same kind.

This was leading nowhere, so I said rather sharply to the leader, "Remove the ladder, please, I am going on." There was a moment's hesitation. "If you do not, we shall. I am going on. I have my orders and will carry them out" – and, in a final argument that drew rather shamefaced apologies, I pointed to the ugly ribbon with a red enamel star, the badge of the French wounded I wore with my other two ribbons, and said, "That was given me in Artois. I was wounded on Vimy and at Notre Dame de Lorette." There was not a soldier in the army who did not know what hell both places were.

The ladder was removed and pulled across the road after me. I drove on, selecting my course according to where I thought I would run into units belonging to the sectors which had been engaged in the last offensive.

I was lucky and gathered a good deal of information. I was stopped next by a machine-gun post mounted alongside the road. With it were two officers who said there were mutinous troops ahead, "*qui ne veulent rien savoir*" ("who will not listen to reason"). "Furthermore they are drunk," and they also told me a good deal of what they had heard about various sectors. According to them, drunkenness had sparked off explosions of despair and misery. And from what they told me I sensed the fear of the men at being thrown once more into the arms of a death fashioned out of barbed wire that this time must enfold those who had so far miraculously escaped it. They had heard that whole units had made for railway stations and rushed trains, demanding to be taken to Paris. Even units of black troops had done so, not knowing what they meant when they shouted, "*A Paris, à Paris!*"

Between them they gave me a terrifying description of these black troops, the Senegalese, who had alarmed me often on the Somme. During the April offensive they had lost, early in the attack, most of their officers whom alone they recognised and obeyed. Without leadership they had lost direction, wandering round in circles, waving their enormous pangas, the formidable *coupe-coupe*, liable to assume that any white man they did not recognise was a German.

Later I ran into a battalion whose officers were in control and who seemed certain of their men. Having explained my mission in connection with the British offensive, I was made welcome as one who could contribute information gleaned earlier which was very interesting news to this group. I told them what I had learnt so far and I listened to them.

They spoke of many cases of regiments refusing to embus for the front, and of others where the 'Internationale' had been sung, giving me the numbers of the units involved.

At another halt I was told that often the men were behaving like industrial strikers, as if the trenches were a place of work that had become distasteful and which consequently they had decided not to visit.

I got back to Paris, following side roads until well away from the army zone, having had only one unpleasant experience, running into a barricade put up by some rather suspicious men, who, conforming with a French atavistic tendency, accused me of being a spy, but saw the logic of the argument that if they had grievances the more people knew of them the better.

Not wanting to impinge too flagrantly on the sphere of the GHQ liaison officers, I kept the special knowledge recently acquired to myself for the moment, and concentrated on gathering information concerning the interior, and this was disquieting enough. Strikes were either taking place or were threatened in several of the neuralgic industrial centres of France.

The government did not appear to be taking strong measures to match those the commander-in-chief was taking in the army zone. And, beginning to feel able to assess the political situation, I warned the CIGS that at the first sign of trouble the Chamber of Deputies would get out of hand.

I expressed the view that in the present crisis the constantly made claim that the British should extend their front and hold a line in proportion to their strength was certain to be revived with renewed vigour, as, indeed, it was.

There were at the time many British troops in camps all down the long lines of communication to Italy; writing from memory, 30,000, perhaps even 50,000 men, were stationed in the neighbourhood of large towns such as Lyons, a very large city of unpredictable moods and prone to disturbances. There were strikes there at the moment and the atmosphere was reported to be explosive. Then came news that there were persistent rumours in Lyons that the British troops there had been sent to fire on the strikers, who were about 3,000 strong. A report to this effect was received by the commander-in-chief, who informed the ambassador.

The consul general at Lyons suggested in considerable alarm that a notice should be inserted in the local papers stating that the British troops were merely in transit.

This was obviously very serious. It was most important not to play into the hands of the revolutionary elements who were on the watch everywhere for incidents which could be represented as intimidation of the civil population by the English or the Senegalese.

A quick visit to some departments of the Ministry of War underlined the extreme danger such reports indicated. Could not the British troops on the lines of communication be confined to camp and not be entrained in the town, which would entail their marching through the streets? People seeing British troops marching through a town would rush off without attempting to find out why they were doing so and report that they were on the way to shoot down the women.

How to have these views acted upon presented a problem, for at this stage I could not venture to make suggestions to GHQ. Fortunately the military Attaché at our Embassy, Colonel Leroy Lewis, was a kind and understanding elderly gentleman. White-haired and boasting a magnificent moustache, a Yeomanry officer with a splendid leg for a boot, generally of shining leather, he could bow to a lady or salute a superior in a way that was the envy of less gifted men. He spoke excellent French, but military problems had hardly come his way, and, in so far as they had, did not appear to have greatly burdened his mind, which was that of a rich and successful business and hunting man. I saw him and explained the problem and, with the weight of the Embassy behind him, he telegraphed to the commander-in-chief recommending that British troops outside the British zone should be confined to their camps and not entrained in towns where there were either strikes or threats of strikes.

This I reported to General Maurice, emphasising the extreme seriousness of the report and the vital importance of acting on it.

Meanwhile I had received additional and very disquieting news of the situation in the French army, in the main in connection with the leave trains.

There were reports of the gravest acts of indiscipline, red flags waved from doors, windows smashed, engines unhitched, station staffs maltreated and on occasion the 'commissaires de gare', the officials charged with discipline at stations, insulted and sometimes beaten.

Horrified officers had heard stations through which leave trains passed echoing with revolutionary songs. All the men on many of the trains seemed to be drunk.

All this was quite frightful, but to me it was just a ghastly ordeal, just one more station we had to pass on the Calvary we must climb on the agonising road to victory.

It never occurred to me that General Pétain and the other French leaders I knew and whom I had seen exercising such a hold on their troops would not re-establish discipline.

That the French army should collapse and refuse to defend France never crossed my mind. These Latins were no Russian moujiks. There will be many executions, I thought grimly, and that was as far as my prognostications went.

It was clear from the timing that it must have been within a very short time of the receipt of my letter of the 7th that a signal was sent me which I received mid-morning on the 9th June ordering me to leave Paris immediately for Abbeville to meet the CIGS at the Officers' Club there.

This I did, and was greatly astonished that Sir William Robertson, who had come from London and had had the Channel to cross, arrived only half an hour after me. He took a bedroom and told me to follow him there. Though it was so long ago, I remember the scene clearly, the burly Wully, the shape of a very large barrel, encircled by his Sam Browne belt, to which he gave slight taps with his hands as he spoke, his drawn-in chin emphasising the incredible thickness of his eyebrows, a veritable zareeba, and above all I remember his voice. I can only remember people well if I can recall their voices and his I shall never forget. It was deep, came up from very low down, in the region of his belt perhaps, rather asthmatic, veiled as if he was speaking through a woollen blanket, and provided a continuous uninterrupted sound as if it were produced by the turning of a handle.

The general effect was one of immense, vital strength, that this was a steam-roller of a man. In a long life in which I have met many leaders of men never have I had to do with one who gave a greater impression of power. He was formidable and very intimidating, but I loved this living lump of granite in spite of his brutal rudeness on occasions, because of his loyalty and his complete faith in and devotion to the army whose honour, one knew, was safe in the hands of this ex-private of dragoons.

Foch said of him, "he does not build high but he builds solid", which was perhaps the correct assessment of his strategic conceptions.

He did not lend himself on this or indeed on any occasion to hero worship. Nothing less like a dandy at his toilet could be conceived. He let himself down grunting into a chair and with much effort removed his leggings and then his boots, a process I watched fascinated, for they were remarkable in that they had bulges, the shape and size of the moulds children used to make mud pies, evidently designed to house large bunions. In the intervals of getting his breath he said, evidently with annoyance, that my report was the first he had heard of the mutinies. I found it

difficult to conceal an astonishment that might have seemed to be
a reflection on the British Mission at French GQG. Wully had
no such scruples and no such reaction. "Do they do nothing beyond waiting to be told what the French want us to believe?" he
growled, and by now, puce in colour although obviously relieved
by the removal of his boots, asked me to tell him in detail what I
had seen and heard. This I did.

Then, having made up his mind on what he wanted me to do,
he told me to return at once to the army zone I had come from
and find out as much more as I could. I was to endeavour to form
an opinion of the extent of the malady and how deep it went
and how the troops affected were reacting to the remedial measures applied – was discipline being re-established? I was then to
return to Paris. I might receive an order to go to London at once,
for it was possible that the Prime Minister might wish to see me.

I left Abbeville immediately for the Aisne front and after motor-
ing all night on very bad roads was lucky enough to find Franchet
d'Esperey fairly early next morning.

He was confident as usual but looked his sternest and I knew
how stern he could be. I had been the British liaison officer to the
5th Army in which he commanded a corps during the latter part
of the great retreat from Mons and Charleroi and the homeric
struggle of the Marne. His army had had then probably the most
important role to play and was weary to death, dispirited beyond
measure, after being driven back over some hundred and fifty
miles of its own country, but he had inspired faith and confidence
in his exhausted troops, kindled hope in their hearts and led them
on to victory. I knew of his inflexible purpose and severity. His
will worked like a steel gin.

If he could not re-establish order no one could.

He knew my position, so there was no necessity to explain to
him that I did not report to the commander-in-chief, or to the
British mission at the GQG.

I explained it was the problem of our troops on the lines of
communication that had led to my wondering what the situation
really was and so I had come back for a quick visit to the army

zone and I told him what I had seen. "By whose permission did
you do that?" he asked. "By yours, *mon général*," I said. "I have
a paper in my pocket signed by you authorising me to visit any
part of the front at any time. And you know I have never mis-
used any information I acquired. Our mission at the GQG has
apparently no inkling of what is happening."

I told him that it was impossible the secret could be kept inde-
finitely and that grossly exaggerated stories would be spread if
great care was not taken. It would be quite wrong not to keep the
British informed in general terms. "They will not expect details
it would be dangerous to formulate, but will expect to be told
whether discipline is being re-established. The British command
knows and has faith in you. They will believe you"; and, as for
myself, I went on to say that having seen the power he could
exercise over the army when necessary, I had no doubt that he
would quell these mutinies which it was becoming clear were the
result of seeing a promised victory receding to regions inaccessible to hope. Hope must be rekindled as he had rekindled it before the Marne.

When I had been attached to the staff of his group of armies he
had been aware of the feelings of the British at the way they had
been treated at and after the Calais Conference.

I thought I was now entitled to say, very gently, though with
Franchet d'Esperey it was more advisable to be frank than tactful,
that it should be recognised that General Nivelle had, to put it
mildly, treated his British allies very shabbily. Just as he had mistaken his successful raids at Verdun for a heaven-inspired new
doctrine of war that conjured away all the obstacles that had
hitherto held up the Allies, so he had mistaken the British nation's
contribution to the war on land for that of a colonial militia which
it was the duty of the French command to control and guide.

Now was not the occasion to count old scores, but it was evident enough that General Nivelle's estimation and treatment of his
allies was as mistaken as his doctrine.

Today it was the British who were successful and it was essential that they keep the enemy occupied on their front, draw his

fire so as to give the French time to recover. These things would be done by us if only because it was to our evident interest that they should be, but surely our effort would be the greater, our co-operation the more complete if the French showed a greater realisation of the humiliations the British had so recently suffered from and under Nivelle's bumptious régime and recognised with a warm and even grateful welcome the brotherly support they were now being offered.

I asked him to allow me to put him a direct and a very important question on the answer to which much might depend.

He knew the deep and respectful confidence long personal experience had led me to place in him. Was he sure the army would recover? I might well be asked to express an opinion and could do so with far greater assurance if he had expressed a view.

He told me he was certain the patriotism and fundamental intelligence of the French soldier would assert itself. It would perhaps be unfortunate if the enemy attacked just now, but there was no sign of his doing so, and even if he did would it in fact be a 'grand malheur'? Even the troops that had given most trouble would certainly resist. They had said they would. He was certain they would. A German attack might well have a sobering effect.

But, he said, it was absolutely essential that discipline should be re-established.

When I pressed him, as I was leaving, for a personal conclusion, he repeated that now his only real fear was that the government would be intimidated by left-wing politicians and would be panicked by threats of strikes into countering the severe measures that were necessary. It was impossible, looking at Franchet d'Esperey, to think of him as being intimidated or frightened by anything. Looking his grimmest, he said once again that he himself had absolutely no doubt that the trouble had been fomented and directed from the interior. There was ample proof of this, but he was satisfied that his method of dealing with mutinous units was the best: allowing parties to climb onto trains or convoys in charge of trustworthy personnel that took them to inaccessible parts of the country and then left them to fend for themselves without shelter or food. There had been no more trouble from any of the units thus treated.

I asked his permission to continue my wanderings in his zone. "Have you not done enough?" he said. But I answered that I had been told to go and see for myself. If I were not allowed to do so it would have an effect that was the contrary of reassuring. After all, this is what I had been doing since 1914 and no one had ever either stopped me or complained of the results.

He agreed, but asked me not to go to Soissons, a big place and no one could tell how the presence of a foreign officer would be received there.

I am grateful to this day for the honour done me by the general in telling me as much as he did. It may well be that he did not himself know that the situation was even worse than he said, and was unaware of the extent of the contamination. He may not have known there had been acts of mutiny all over France, from Bordeaux to Nantes and Limoges, and that a hundred and ten units belonging to fifty-four divisions, more than half the divisions constituting the French army, had mutinied.

I am glad in any case that I did not know, for if I had it may well be that I could not have maintained an optimism that proved to be useful.

Had I known the scope of the disease I could but have reported it, and this might have had very grave consequences.

Having located the whereabouts of some formations where I had friends or acquaintances, I went my way.

Officers I knew were not surprised to see me and spoke freely enough. The greetings I received from past acquaintances were warm and friendly. They were even more anxious to hear my news than I was to hear theirs. How were things going? they asked.

It was reassuring to note that I found no trace of defeatism, no despair at the present turn of affairs, but confidence that this was a passing phase, that Pétain, with his severity and the respect and affection in which he was held by the troops, would soon re-establish order.

It was striking how much the need for severity and strictly enforced discipline was dwelt upon, and generals who enforced it were much praised.

I heard of how some troops ordered up to the line had obeyed, but when passing other troops had baaed like sheep, implying they were on their way to the slaughterhouse.

"Your turn for the turnstiles," was a form of greeting that had found favour among men watching others embus for the front.

Those who told me this, whilst not underestimating the dangers such an attitude presented, tended on the whole to attribute it to a kind of sour self-pity, a way of jeering at your own misfortunes which is characteristic of some regions of France, notably Paris. And as I listened I remembered both reading and being told that the troops engaged in the uneven struggle against the Germans in the Franco-Prussian War of 1870 used to sing songs to gay tunes describing themselves as being driven out to inevitable death like rats,[1] a form of humour, a kind of self-pity which has never manifested itself in our island, but which, it should be noted, never prevented these rather pathetic cynics in uniform from fighting when called upon to do so, even if dimmed hopes sapped the vigour of their offensive spirit. But it is true that for a long time now the *furia francesa* had disappeared, to be replaced by a stoical endurance our forebears had believed the French to be incapable of.

[1] *Nous partons,*
  Ton, ton,
  Comme des moutons,
  Comme des moutons,
  Pour la boucherie,
  Pour la boucherie,
  Nous aimons
  Pourtant la vie.
  Mais nous partons,
  Ton, ton,
  Pour la boucherie,
  On nous massacrera,
  Ra, ra,
  Comme des rats,
  Ah! que Bismarck rira!

I got to Paris in the early afternoon of the 13th June and found a message to call up General Maurice on my arrival. He told me to report at the War Office next morning at 10 am. This meant some pretty fast driving over bad roads. I arrived at Boulogne in the night and produced my most precious document, one instructing the Navy to get me across the Channel at any time I requested a passage.

The demand was received without enthusiasm. It was pointed out that the Royal Navy was not a post chaise establishment and furthermore that as it was low tide the danger from mines was that much the greater. But they got me across, and at Dover I was allowed to ride on an engine part of the way to London, arriving in time to have a bath and shave at the Cavalry Club before keeping my appointment.

At the War Office I gave the CIGS a short account of what I had gathered on the Aisne front, and, as we walked over to Downing Street, he said: "Say what you have to say, answer questions and keep to the facts you are sure of." At No. 10 he was called into the Cabinet room and I was kept waiting for some time in a room outside. Then he came out to fetch me. By then if there had been Ministers in the Cabinet room most of them had dispersed. I recognised Lord Robert Cecil talking to someone sitting at the table, and Colonel Hankey, the cabinet's secretary, whom I knew well, in conversation with someone else, both standing, and there was the Prime Minister.

Mr Lloyd George beckoned me into a window recess giving on to the garden. He looked enquiringly at me and I am sure I gazed at him with curiosity and certainly in some anxiety, possibly in some fear of the alarming tricks army messes spoke of as lurking up both his sleeves.

He was obviously weighing me up.

I do not think he remembered that on one occasion when he and John Simon had visited the front in the Arras sector, probably in 1915, I had sat between him and General Foch at lunch, a miserable position which despite every effort on my part to translate both French and English with my mouth

full led to my having to leave an unusually good meal half
eaten.

It was evident that the look that ricochetted over me to the
CIGS was not a friendly one. It would in fact be no exaggeration
to say it was the contrary.

"Colonel Spears," he began, "you have been given your present position because presumably the military authorities believe
you are thoroughly familiar with the French army. Is that so?" I
answered that I had been attached to it since the beginning of the
war. I then remembered, and remembered vividly, as a pain is
remembered, that not very long before, soon after my appointment to Paris, Colonel Repington, the celebrated military corre-
spondent of *The Times*, had come to see me. Unused to the press
or anything to do with it, I had been very much on my guard for
fear he might try to draw from me some information I should not
have disclosed, but instead he had given me political news from
London which was entirely unexpected and very startling: this
was that the Conservative members of the government trusted the
Prime Minister not at all. 'You are no doubt aware," said Repington, "of the peace feelers that are being put out from a number of
directions, notably by Austria. Well, there are people in London
who feel that Lloyd George might snatch at an opportunity to
conclude a separate peace at his Allies' expense, and would do so
if a part of any of the armies of the coalition collapsed," and he
had asked me how solid I thought the French really were after
their failed offensive, a question I had answered very convinc-
ingly, I hoped; but now, face to face with the Prime Minister, his
question made me remember Colonel Repington's statement, and
something very like panic seized me as it dawned on me that my
report might furnish Mr Lloyd George with just the pretext he
needed, according to Repington, to fade out of the war. Subsequent knowledge of the Prime Minister made me realise that such
apprehensions were completely unjustified.

Standing in that window recess, these and other thoughts flashed
across my mind. I was aware of being scrutinised, but I was examining my interlocutor myself, and I noted that the Prime Minister

was snappy and concluded that this was perhaps caused by his evident hostility to the CIGS. He certainly eyed him with extreme distaste, an expression that seemed to be amplified as its waves struck against the solid bulk of his chief military adviser.

This attitude of Mr Lloyd George must have struck me as a weakness for, instead of intimidating me further, it gave me considerable encouragement.

Glancing at Wully Robertson I felt the whole strength of the army beside me; so long as one hung on to that solid rugged boulder no political blizzard could sweep one away.

As the Prime Minister gave me the impression he was going to begin to cross-examine me, another fear seized me.

Any description I could give Mr Lloyd George, any picture I might draw for him of what I had seen, of the incidents I had heard of at first hand, however truthfully told, would certainly mislead him; having not the least knowledge of the French army (or of any army for the matter of that) he would draw the wrong conclusions from my words, see pictures that were not those I was attempting to draw, and above everything else he could not possibly begin to understand the French soldier's temperament, or grasp his incredible recuperative powers, and so I resolved to avoid getting involved in detailed descriptions. The Prime Minister helped me in this for he said suddenly, "Colonel Spears, you have been appointed to a responsible position by the military authorities. I understand you have just visited some sections of the French army where there has been serious trouble. This is a very serious situation. The question I am asking you is a grave one, I presume you realise how grave: Is the French army going to recover? You should be able to express a positive opinion."

The bluntness, the directness of the question took me aback. It was certainly better than being asked to describe what I had seen, but it struck me as surprising to be asked to foretell the conclusion of a tale as yet only half told.

I had not expected to be asked to do more than recount what had so far occurred.

Mr Lloyd George was looking at me keenly. "Well?" he asked.

Then again: "Will the French army recover or not, that is the question."

I was flustered and must have seemed stupid or evasive, for the Prime Minister now pressed me like a terrier. "I am sure it will," I said, and told him that General Pétain was a wonderful leader, one in whom the men had confidence, and a great disciplinarian as well.

It seemed to be of immense importance to convince the Prime Minister. The fear of failing to do so was frightening. It could not even be contemplated.

I was sure now, desperately sure, that General Pétain could nurse his army back to health were he but given the time to do so, and this the British could do by carrying out the attack they had planned. But these, I felt, were not considerations that could be mentioned to Mr Lloyd George, they would only raise more doubts in his mind. It would not give him encouragement and confidence to suggest that the French army must look to the British commanders, in whom he had no confidence, for its salvation.

So I tried to make him understand the immense power the commander of an army trusted by the troops could exercise over them if they felt he could lead them to success while being sparing of their lives, and I was certain the French soldiers felt this about Pétain, for I had lived through some of his brilliant operations with his troops. So I asserted that the French army would soon recover its morale and its vigour, for its powers of recuperation under good leadership were seemingly miraculous. I reminded the Prime Minister how it had fought at the Marne after suffering a continuous series of shattering defeats. The French soldier was turning out to be in many ways the opposite of what we had believed him to be. Far from being fickle and volatile he was proving to be stable, staunch and tenacious.

Suddenly Mr Lloyd George's voice changed. It was now bland, persuasive, with a musical undertone. His words, like birds about to glide into flight, gave the impression they were on the point of changing into musical notes. But they did not. Being unmusical

I would not have understood if they had. A worm falling into a pot of honey might feel as I did, at first delighted at the sweet smoothness of my environment, then receiving a violent shock to find things were not what they seemed, for the Prime Minister was saying, "Will you give me your word of honour as an officer and a gentleman that the French army will recover?"

Completely taken aback, I was simply furious. It seemed evident that to ask such a question, to request a man to pledge his word of honour on a matter still in the future and likely to remain so, simply meant that the questioner did not know the meaning of either officer or gentleman and could indeed only have the most imprecise views concerning the meaning, purpose and obligations of giving a word of honour, and I said so. I have a picture of myself gibbering with rage, for I told the Prime Minister he could not understand the meaning of the words officer and gentleman to put such a question. Feeling desperate now, terrified of seeming to evade the question, anxious to put my maximum stake on the advice I was giving, I told the Prime Minister I would stake my life on what I was saying. "Call Hankey and he can take down what I say. You can have me shot if I am mistaken. I will stake my life on it," I repeated and then added stubbornly, "But not my word of honour." And then repeated once more: "The French army under Pétain will surely recover."

"That will do," said Wully and I followed him as he walked out of the room.

I remember feeling a bit dizzy in the street and rather ashamedly steadying myself against the railings of Number 10.[1]

I was soon back in Paris, haunted by the fear I might not have rightly assessed the situation of the French army.

In the days which followed my return I kept in as close touch as was possible with M. Painlevé, the Minister for War. I did not,

[1] I must add that Mr Lloyd George, who might have resented my outburst, never did so either during the war or in after years when I was myself in the House of Commons.

nor could I possibly know everything that was going on, nor all
the aspects of his problem, but I gained some inkling of the weight
of the moral responsibility that rested on the shoulders of this
modest and just man.

It can never have been the lot of a kindlier man to have a voice
in the decision as to whether an individual soldier should live or
die. In after years Painlevé often spoke to me of the agonising
duty of attempting to weigh the evidence of mutiny or insubordination against the excuses a kind and imaginative heart could
conjure up. I knew at the time something of what was involved,
but perhaps only appreciated later what he had gone through
every hour of the short agony each condemned man experienced
before his time came of an early morning. The minister knew full
well the commander-in-chief hated taking the final irrevocable
decision as much as he himself did, yet he fought and argued every
point in a condemned man's favour as if he were struggling to
pull a living creature out of the clutches of a bloodthirsty fiend.[1]

He could not have done this with such tireless vigour had he not
known he was pleading with a man who perhaps suffered more
than he did because of the weight of the harness of the stern and
harrowing duty that was his to carry. And so both men, night
after night, spoke to each other either over the telephone, or
when the tired minister walked rather uncertainly, after driving
from Paris, into the commander-in-chief's room at Compiègne,
having dropped everything to discuss the small matter of one
man's life, when the lives of scores of thousands were at stake and

---

[1] Such was the case when the minister had pleaded with the commander-in-
chief for the life of a corporal of under twenty who had seen his father shot by
the Germans earlier in the war, who had fought bravely, but had led a rebellion
in his unit. The minister tried until midnight to extract a pardon from the
commander-in-chief on his behalf, but failed. The crime was too flagrant, the
boy corporal had only been prevented by the intervention of others from shooting an officer. General Pétain was adamant. The sentence must be carried out.
But the minister in Paris could not sleep. He got up at three in the morning and
had the commander-in-chief called to make a final plea which failed. There are
those who would rather die themselves than condemn others to die, but those
on whom this responsibility bears so heavily and yet carry it out set a great
example to their countrymen.

the fate of France herself was in the balance. On the whole the
moral burden that rested on the general was the heavier, for the
ultimate responsibility was his, and the minister knew that he
could unleash the full torrent of his sentimentality on the soldier
who would, he knew, resist all appeals if he knew it was his duty
to do so. He could therefore indulge in putting forward every
plea for mercy, knowing that the other would enforce only the
minimum retribution essential to the army's return to moral
health.

But when all is said and in the light of after knowledge there
can be no doubt that it was the re-establishment of the *Cours
Martiales* that restored discipline at one brutal stroke. These had
been suppressed in 1916 and no one had been gladder than I, for I
had seen something of how they had worked and I hated them.
They had been proved to be often unjust and were too much even
for the French outlook in such matters, which is prepared to
accept many encroachments both on justice and on freedom if the
safety of the nation is involved.[1]

General Pétain and his commanders were proved to have been
right in insisting on the re-establishment of discipline at all costs.
The government's decree setting up military courts promulgated
on the 9th June was made known to the army next day, the 10th
June. From that date there was not a single case of collective disobedience entailing the death penalty.

I was not aware then that it was only because the situation of the
army was described as desperate by the commander-in-chief and
accepted to be such by the government that these peace-loving
radical politicians were driven to support measures repugnant

[1] *Les Cours Martiales*, established by decree in September 1914, consisted of
three officers who could be appointed on the spot, convene the court immediately and try the accused, who if found guilty was punished without delay.
There was no appeal from their decisions.

It should be explained that these *Cours Martiales* were not legally re-established in 1917 since this would have entailed legislation involving parliamentary discussions revealing the terrible situation of the army, but the procedure
of the *Conseils de Guerre* which took their place was so shortened and curtailed as
to assimilate them to the *Cours Martiales*; in particular the President of the Republic abdicated his power of reprieve into the hands of the commander-in-chief.

alike to their convictions and instincts. Had I been fully aware of this I would have been in an agony of doubt about the report I had made to the Prime Minister in London.

As it was I could only guess what Painlevé's problems really were from my meetings with him, which grew more frequent with time as I learnt to appreciate a kind of man hitherto quite outside my experience.

Painlevé was a man of the Left, a radical but not a socialist, a great mathematician whose heart sometimes seemed to hesitate and lose its way as it followed his mind, for ever exploring the paths of the stars, measuring the inconceivable distances of their infinite ways.

He was as great a patriot as any of the generals who were now theoretically ruled by him, but his love of France was not that of the heroic legends that live for ever embodied in Rude's statuary on the Arc de Triomphe. It was that of the family grouped round an oil lamp of an evening, the children doing their home-work, the father reading his paper while his wife knits, it was that of the workshop but not that of the *estaminet*.

On the 19th June I wrote to General Maurice once more. I was deeply concerned by the responsibility of the report I had made to the Prime Minister, but far more so by the importance of attempt-ing to assess the real state of the French army.

I reported on this occasion that I had felt it my duty to return to the northern group of armies to find out how matters now stood, and that I had seen many officers, from General Franchet d'Esperey and the army group commanders down to battalion commanders in the line. As a result of this visit I had to admit that the mutinies had been far more serious than I had believed, but I was given to understand that the trouble was now well in hand.

Some details worth noting were told me. I was informed, for instance, that the most serious trouble occurred in the 5th Divi-sion of the III Corps, but the whole corps had been involved. (It was the 5th Division which, under General Mangin, took Fort Douaumont at Verdun.)

I was given the numbers of several corps and divisions affected, the 14th and 41st Division of the VII Corps (which had attacked very gallantly on the 16th April), also General Pétain's XXXIII and XXI Corps, but it was painful to hear that the XX Corps, the pride of the whole army, had also been contaminated, fortunately only slightly. Strangely enough two corps with excellent reputations, the III and the XXI, both having had long periods of rest previous to the outbreak, gave serious trouble, lending colour to the belief that agents of subversion had been active in their billets and rest camps. I reported that there might well be more incidents that I had not heard of. There were. It was only much later that I learnt that over half the total of the French army, that is fifty-four divisions, had been involved. One hundred and fifty-one cases of collective rebellion were investigated. Of these seventy-four proved to be of real gravity. Nearly all had taken place in the Aisne region behind the Chemin-des-Dames.

I gave the following as examples of some incidents I was told of by officers who had witnessed them.

A battalion of the 370th Regiment scattered, was rounded up by cavalry but, defying their escorts, took possession of a village, then elected their own officers, who maintained strict discipline.

The village was surrounded by loyal troops, consisting in the main of artillery and cavalry, and the mutineers were starved. The inhabitants were allowed out twice a day when meals were given them.

One evening the mutineers offered to surrender but were told they could only do so next morning at a given time, by groups of ten, unarmed. This they did, marching in step, beautifully turned out and, an almost unbelievable touch at the time – in the circumstances – with their boots polished. Each squad was halted and scrutinised by their own officers and security men; they pointed out the men they suspected of being the leaders. They were fallen out, packed into a waiting train and taken to the place where Courts Martial sat permanently. No one knew what had happened to them after that. I gathered that the brave and resigned attitude of the mutineers had deeply impressed the troops that had beleaguered them, and once again I was told it would be unwise to rely on their performing the same task again. Censored letters revealed the deep disquiet of the men at being thus employed and some wrote they would refuse to obey similar orders if repeated.

The mutiny had evidently taken many forms and the methods employed had varied greatly.

Two regiments of the 5th Division, proving insubordinate, were sent to the XI Corps, all stations on the way guarded by cavalry. At the time of my visit the cavalry still held the stations and the regiments were still held by the XI Corps.

There was the case of a battalion attacking the motor convoy which was to drive them to the trenches, threatening the drivers and its own officers, and another in which a battalion commander was pursued by his men. And there were many other incidents; no one had been killed, nor had there been any wounded, but I was able to see for myself that in many cases the inhabitants had been terrified. Very many had been those who had turned an honest penny by selling illicit alcohol to the men, but they had been sorry indeed when they saw bands of drunken soldiers, rejecting all discipline, wandering about the villages and towns.

The military authorities were more convinced than ever that the whole trouble had been organised by the syndicates, the CGT (Confédération Générale du Travail), that the time had been well selected, taking advantage of the discouragement of the army and the effect of the Russian Revolution. It was felt that the movement might have contaminated the whole army (it almost did) but had failed principally owing to some premature mutinies which broke out before the whole plan was ripe.

All insisted on how the action of the disaffected men had resembled a strike. I was on the whole well received, often with curiosity. I generally expected to get on best with cavalrymen, being one myself, for there were always common grounds of interest, horses, but this occasion was an exception, and the officers were neither friendly nor very polite.

These aristocratic men were bitterly humiliated by the fact of the mutinies, a slur on the bravery which was to most of them the epitome of France, the France they understood and accepted. And here they were, acting as gendarmes to these misguided hordes, and here was a foreign officer viewing the whole scene, spying on them was what some of them no doubt thought, although it may have occurred to individuals that in view of our involvement in the present campaign we were entitled to keep ourselves informed of events in the main theatre.

There had been occasions when I had witnessed with amazed and rather admiring interest the ease with which some French aristocrats had, with inherited dexterity, reduced an intruder to abashed silence, and that with the most exquisite expertise, the most perfect politeness. But it was unpleasant to have, for the first and last time, this technique applied to me.

A symptom of the depth of the anxiety felt by senior officers was the earnestness with which I was asked by several whether the British government would bring pressure on their ally to ensure that such coercive measures as were necessary were taken so as to ensure that a recurrence of the trouble in the interior would be impossible.

The very direct questions I put to senior officers whom I knew personally were answered in a way calculated to make me feel we must either place our faith in Pétain or accept that we must assume more of the burden of fighting the war ourselves. But the concensus of opinion expressed seemed to be that the trouble would be quelled in two or three weeks, although no one could yet say how soon the troops affected would be fit to attack again or when the army as a whole would have regained its moral health.

As an indication of the state of affairs, I noted that a forthcoming attack in the St Gobain sector was to be carried out by the cavalry.

My own conclusions were that while the mutinies had been far more serious than I had at first thought the situation was now well in hand.

But putting an end to a mutiny and transforming the men in-involved into good fighting troops were two totally different things. The French army, I was certain, could not withstand a recurrence of similar troubles.

I believed at the time, as did the high-ranking officers who informed me, that the repressive measures taken by the command were far more severe than they actually were. This was due to a merciful deception conceived by General Pétain whereby men condemned to death by Court Martial and reprieved disappeared completely, all their comrades believing they had indeed been shot, whereas they had been sent to some distant place of detention in Morocco or Indo-China where they remained incommunicado for a long period.

The number of executions attributable to collective disobedience was remarkably low: twenty-three, out of an army of four million men, more than half of whose divisions had been affected; these are M. Painlevé's figures.

General Pétain states that there were fifty-five executions, but that only thirty of these related to the "re-establishment of morale", which means that twenty-five were executed for looting, highway robbery and similar crimes calling for the death penalty in time of war, while only thirty executions were carried out on men guilty of collective disobedience.

It may be that the disparity between the figures of the soldier and the politician is due to the fact that two men in M. Painlevé's list seemed to have been tried on charges of both mutiny and looting and that the condemnation was attributable more to the second than to the first crime.

There were other sanctions. Detachments from units which had given trouble were quietly shipped to distant dependencies. Rumour had it that their destinations were not salubrious nor renowned for their amenities, but I do not know. It is what one would have expected.

On two or three occasions I saw in the streets of Paris small canvas-covered brakes drawn by two horses, close behind which rode two mounted gendarmes. In these brakes, seated low and peering over the low door were men I knew to have been condemned by Court Martial. They were, I believe, on their way to some overseas destination, but they may have thought they were being taken to the fort where they would be executed next day. Although it is so long ago their faces haunt me still. The Inquisition sometimes chalked the faces of its victims on their way to the stake. One such face seemed to peer at me out of the back of one of the carriages, snow white it seemed, and horribly grinning, a mask of intolerable pain clamped onto lunatic features. I still feel as if on that occasion I had seen a trolley-load of lost souls being driven at a fast trot down into hell.

From the moment he had assumed the supreme command General Pétain, his line of conduct clearly in his mind, had set about his task of healing, which entailed some drastic surgery, with an indomitability of purpose which would have been impossible had he had the slightest doubt of the soundness of the remedies he proposed to apply.

I, the observer, watched with intense admiration this sure-handed military surgeon standing over the torn body of the French army which, mangled and tortured nearly to death by bad generalship and insensitive handling, was now in the course of being cured by inspired leadership and humane understanding.

The first and overriding quality which he revealed was the power to control completely his physical being which, seemingly without effort, dominated fatigue and dispensed with sleep. He was on the road day and night until he had visited every one of the contaminated divisions. His second great asset was the simplicity of his doctrine, which was that whatever happened and at whatever cost discipline must be re-established, immediately and in all its rigour. The first victims of this axiom were the officers who invoked as a pretext for their pusillanimous conduct the fact that, as the movement was a general one, it was difficult to detect its leaders. To this excuse Pétain retorted icily that: "Nothing is easier than to transform a collective act of disobedience into individual rebellion. It suffices to give an order to a few men, preferably to the notoriously difficult characters, and, should they refuse to obey, have them immediately arrested and handed over to a military court to be dealt with without any delay whatsoever."

Without ceasing to control the army as a whole, Pétain, after visiting the affected divisions, added to his stupendous task by visiting all the others, and in doing so displayed a unique faculty of making those he spoke to feel that they had found a father in the ideal sense, an older man who understood the problems of each and was bent on helping to solve them, but one who, fathering so many, was bound to be severe, cutting out any elements which might corrupt the rest.

He laid it down that officers, NCO's and men from each battalion and indeed of each company should be represented at his meetings.

The commander-in-chief's aim was to establish at once a feeling of confidence in those he addressed. Sometimes standing in an open field, as likely as not leaning against the bonnet of his car, he described the war situation, asserting that the boundless resources of the United States in men and material must inevitably bring victory, it was just a question of holding out, of hanging on until the stream flowing from America swelled into a spate.

Using expressions comprehensible to his audience, he cast the light of his clear appreciation of the situation on the various sectors of the front in France and Italy, and then spoke of the other theatres, and the men to whom he spoke, until that moment only vaguely informed of what was involved in the war beyond their own narrow field of vision and experience, suddenly felt they were at the hub of it, the confidants of the commander-in-chief whose word they had that they only had to hold on to win. Every man who heard him grew in his own estimation, as presently did all his comrades to whom he recounted his astonishing experience.

No one realised better than General Pétain that in the final result the conduct of a unit is a reflection of the officers' powers of leadership, and he knew how important it was as a general rule never to weaken the authority of an officer by reproving him before his men, yet he achieved the extraordinary effect, whilst not damaging the hierarchical structure of the army, of castigating some officers so severely that their men wept for them, and asked him to be less severe. I do not imagine that the officers thus casti-gated remained with their units (some were reduced in rank), but I heard from those who had been present on such occasions of the extraordinarily uplifting effect these meetings had on the men.

It was hard to withhold sympathy for some of the infantry officers. Most of them were not fitted by position or training to act as leaders. Ex-NCO's, they had been promoted by German bullets which had caused the vacancies which, of necessity, they had been promoted to fill.

General Pétain had always read in advance the reports concern-ing the engagements and casualties of the division he was addres-sing and had details of acts of bravery both of units and of in-dividuals. These he commented upon and rewarded on the spot. He had a plentiful supply of *Médailles Militaires, Croix de Guerre* and Legions of Honour which he gave on the recommendation of the responsible officers without any more formality than noting the name of the recipient. He then distributed lavishly small pre-sents, packets of tobacco and cigarettes, and pipes inscribed with a facsimile of his signature (an idea inherited from Joffre). These were greatly prized.

The commander-in-chief would then inspect cookhouses, cross-examine cooks, often order better cooked food, and inspect rest billets, concerning which he often had much to say. Then he would examine the leave rosters and make sure leave was granted with complete fairness, for he well knew that nothing could cause more heart-burning than postponed or cancelled leave.

An incident will illustrate the effect Pétain's methods had on the army.

On the occasion of one of these visits, a private soldier asked leave to speak to him.

He had had no leave for eighteen months, his wife was ill and very anxious to see him.

The man went on leave. A few months later Pétain inspected the same division and recognised the man. Calling him out of the ranks he asked how his wife was. "My going did her good, but she told me to do something about you, *mon Général*, that I dare not tell you." "Why shouldn't you tell me? Out with it," said Pétain.

"She told me to embrace you, *mon Général*." "And what is stopping you?" said Pétain. And there, in front of the astonished troops, a private was seen to kiss the commander-in-chief on both cheeks.

Stories such as this spread through the armies with astonishing speed and very soon the leader was enshrined as a titular deity. How much did not Napoleon owe to tales such as that of his taking up the gun of the sleeping sentry and carrying out his duty for him?

In a very short time the whole army became aware that everything to do with welfare had vastly improved, and, quite rightly, attributed this to General Pétain. The men going on leave were no longer packed into trains with broken windows. Hitherto there had been nowhere to sit down under shelter at many railway halts, and there had been no one to organise the journeys and advise bewildered and bedraggled men how to reach their often distant destinations. Now all this was changed. Every effort was made to help the weary man homeward so that he should not lose a minute of his precious leave. Attractive reception centres were created and the soldier released from the front felt at last that he was being treated otherwise than as an escaped convict. No longer did you hear quips such as "Even pigs are driven to market".

How Pétain re-established the morale of the French army is a subject that should be carefully studied by all commanders. But it should be remembered that he was dealing with Frenchmen, whose qualities and faults are not easily comparable with those of men of other nations.

You could not superimpose Pétain's remedies on another set of circumstances or another army as you would a transparency on a plan and expect similar results.

If it were your purpose to study and understand the French soldier you should not commit the mistake of assuming he had much in common with the French civilian.

As a civilian he had been critical and resentful of authority, mistrustful of his employer whom he suspected, generally with some justification, of being bent on taking advantage of him. Hardworking and abstemious, such pleasures as he got out of life in his limited sphere were simple. He had within him all the elements that make a good citizen.

As a soldier he stood up to the very hard army life because it was a traditional and inescapable ordeal that every generation of his countrymen bore in turn.

As he put on his uniform he knew he was falling under a strong discipline that was probably harsh and might well be unjust, but that was a matter of luck, what his NCO's would turn out to be, and this, after all, was the same for all the other lads of his age: a sacrifice for France.

One great compensation was that he had shed all responsibility, and the hold of his family, generally strong in France, had relaxed. All he had to do now was to obey a new and exacting authority, used however to dealing with generations of young Frenchmen, severe in matters of routine, but indulgent to the young male just aware of his manhood. The young soldier felt himself enveloped in an atmosphere in which patriotism and discipline tended to assume the same aspect. The flag, France, 'honneur et patrie' the universal motto, learning how to repel the enemy, all this blended in his mind as it was hammered into his head by the irresistible, the irrepressible roll of the drums. He had always been taught to love France and it was his deepest instinct to do so, just as he loved his mother, naturally.

France to him was his village nestling cosily into its province, and France was its background; the army was his province still, for his regiment was recruited from it. His fellows had the same accent as he had. This he could not perceive as a characteristic of his own voice but could recognise it in others. Other regiments spoke French too but it was not the same thing, they had a rather funny way of saying things, slow or heavy, not to mention the men of Provence who were so funny and whom everyone enjoyed imitating.

Here in the army the great companionship of men, deeply felt by all the human races, had the effect it always had of binding soldiers into a great fraternity, loyal to itself and deeply comforting. Had it not been for this primordial instinct none of the armies involved in the Great War would have held out. But with the French it did not go as deep as it does with the British, who, when things go badly, instinctively hold together more stoutly and fight together shoulder to shoulder. A body of the more individualistic Frenchmen whose splendid qualities of quick initiative and rapid movement serve them so well in battle tends to disintegrate when nerves are overstrained. We have no words in our language to express the '*sauve qui peut*' – 'let all flee who can' – an expression not unknown among French forces, even those who have fought very well. And again the cry '*nous sommes trahis*" which had often spread panic in French armies, denotes a proclivity to blame others for defeat which is incompatible with the solid cohesion which on most occasions is the characteristic of British troops in retreat.

The French soldier, freed of his civilian attributions, emerges as a singularly simple, confiding, affectionate man, ready to trust his leaders, easy to lead, appreciative of kindness. In civil life intensely responsive to outward forms of politeness, ready to resent any expression of superiority, the military forms of greeting are accepted by the soldier: the sealed pattern of the army's social behaviour, the salute, the joined heels, the invariable greeting '*mon*' to a superior, '*mon*' *capitaine*, '*mon*' *général*, appeal alike to the Frenchman's sense of propriety, of good order and of politeness. All this tends to create a universality to which he responds. But the army itself, its organisation and its purpose, was necessarily impersonal, a machine for transmuting two or three hundred thousand anonymous civilians each year into an equal number of anonymous soldiers. This did not allow for frills or niceties when so much had to be done in so short a time, when the stupid, the clumsy and the lazy, together with the clever and the agile, had to be pressed into the same mould, which left little room for sentiment or cultivating personal relationships between officers and men.

General Pétain, the dour infantryman of hard northern peasant stock, understood the French soldier and staked everything on his belief in his fundamental patriotism, confident that, on reflection, he would realise that to give up the struggle would be a betrayal of the hosts who had died to carry on the war so far.

His point of view was that of another French officer whom I had quoted to him once in Artois, Duval by name.[1]

Duval had said, "I am of country stock, of the tough Cévennes protestant mountain folk, we are hard-headed realists and had learnt the lesson of the Napoleonic wars and of our defeat by the Germans in 1870. The odds for victory were against us, we knew that, but we had acutely suffered over the years from German bullying, we had seen that the Germans lost no opportunity of humiliating us, of spitting in our faces, so that when the call came in August 1914 the whole country rose as one man, glad, even if it meant dying, of the chance to cleanse the face of France of all those outrages, to redeem all those humiliations.

"And so we flung ourselves at the throat of Germany in deadly earnest. There was no fanfare as in 1870. We all staked our lives in a furious and unanimous determination to shake off the shackles our defeat had riveted on our limbs."

"I agree with that," said Pétain when I told him.

And I who had lived those hours in 1914 knew it was true, knew that every man in the army realised that on his personal steadfastness and endurance depended the survival of France, that the immense casualty lists which lengthened every hour, every minute of the day and night, increased his responsibility to so many dead, for if he gave way their colossal sacrifice would have been in vain.

[1] A major in charge of the 2ième Bureau (Intelligence) of the 5th Army during the Marne, he later became a general and head of the Historical Section of the army.

General Pétain, by force of circumstances, and also because it was his instinct to do so, introduced an entirely new method of treatment of the soldier within the military machine. His conception of the army was of a great number of individuals brought together by the necessity of national defence into disciplined units, but individuals all the same, instead of the accepted theory of a yearly human crop to be poured into moulds from which they emerged as automatons to be moved about maps according to whatever was the military theory of the moment.

The battle of the Marne has often been spoken of as a miracle. The sudden transformation of beaten weary masses of men into aggressive armies was indeed a miracle, the miracle of hope rekindled burning out despair in a million hearts.

But General Pétain's achievement was in fact a greater, a far greater miracle than the Marne. To turn soldiers who did not feel beaten but only indignant, as indignant as extreme fatigue would allow, and unleash them at an enemy they had been longing to get at for weeks, was as easy as opening the gates to a football final crowd compared with transmuting mutineers into soldiers, changing insolent strikers into disciplined troops, converting bands of drunks into steady battalions. And it was no superficial change. Carefully nursed, re-educated in the tactics of war as they were then, encouraged by being engaged in extremely well-thought-out and meticulously prepared attacks in which artillery had done all those things the infantry had for so long prayed for but prayed for in vain, such as effectively cutting paths through the barbed wire, putting down barrages that preceded the attacking waves instead of pounding them or leaving them far behind; rested, now well looked after, confident in the leadership, the French soldier was transformed.

The modest successes of the latter part of 1917 made possible the victories of 1918 which in turn made the French army a reincarnation of what it had been in the great periods of its history.

It was as if the spirit of Valmy, which had hurled the ragged levies of the First Republic across its frontiers, rekindled in 1914 but killed by a slow strangled death in the mud of the trenches, had been reborn.

It was a small flickering light at first, but presently grew very strong until it filled every man's heart, now cleansed of fear, with hope.

I realised this fulfilment when I was present at the entry of the French troops into Strasbourg after the Armistice in 1918. I stood near General Pétain when he heard the first Mass celebrated in French in the cathedral after an interval of forty-five years, and stood just behind one-armed General Gouraud when he reviewed the French army as it marched into the capital of Alsace.

I have seen many magnificent parades in my life, including the celebration of victory by the Allied troops in the Champs Elysées in Paris, but none has ever moved me as deeply as the entry of the French troops into Strasbourg. The spirit was superb and illuminated all those faces deeply marked by war; the trumpets, shrill and harsh, tore the ears as they blared their cadenced notes into hearts that swelled in pain as if they would burst in the pangs of giving birth to a new conception, that of victory, while the drums, row upon row of them in loud, muffled, hurried, pounding throbs, were as the heart beats marking the stride of armies on their relentless revengeful march to occupy the land of the enemy they had defeated.

The parade over, deeply moved, I told General Gouraud that I was overwhelmed by the miracle I had witnessed, that of the resurrection of an army that had been threatened by death in 1917. And I told him I had had a kind of vision as I stood near him watching the regiments go by: I had felt that behind him, all the way up to Heaven, there was tier upon tier of men, endless rows of them, all the dead of the war, and that an immense satisfaction prevailed among them as they looked down on his army, for they knew they had not died in vain, for this army of the end of the war was better than had been theirs of the beginning. And he told me that he had had very much the same impression, and that he had felt sure that his mother, who had died very recently, was standing close behind him, deeply happy at what she saw.

I told General Pétain of this, and later recalled the Strasbourg review several times. My theme was that the attitude of Frenchmen, both military and political, in the years after the war, was mistaken. They shunned the subject of the mutinies, looked embarrassed if it as much as peeped over the fringe of a conversation, evidently feeling it was a topic best avoided, something to be ashamed of. It was hardly mentioned in their official history of the war, whereas I contended the story should be a matter of great pride, in the same category as the action of the officer in General Maunoury's army who at the dawn of the Marne, mortally wounded and surrounded by stricken men, on seeing the Germans advance, arose, seized a rifle and shouted, "*Debout les morts!*" – "Up the dead!"

Time passed. One day I received a note from Marshal Pétain saying he would like to see me the next time I was in Paris. He handed me a folder containing his narrative of the mutinies with his manuscript notes on the typescript, and told me he would like me to publish it. As usual, his remarks were short, clear and to the point. He said in effect that as I had been so long at the point of junction between the French and British Armies and had lived through so many of the battles of the war with the French, sharing their good as well as their bad fortunes, he would like me to write the story of the mutinies and here were his own notes to enable me to do so.

To say that I was taken aback would be an understatement. In spite of the explanation he had given me, I asked why he had selected me for this honour. He said that he had come to the conclusion that an Englishman would tell the story more objectively than a Frenchman, who would find it difficult not to become involved in controversy, to defend or condemn one set of people rather than another.

Presently, having thought the matter over, I decided that to tell a coherent story I must include all the events of 1917 in my narrative, since the mutinies were deeply rooted in the politico-mili-

tary problems which developed so catastrophically at the beginning of the year. But the task proved to be a formidable one for a
man who had parliamentary duties to perform and was also
earning his living in business.

By 1939 I had written quite a long book, but the mutinies of
1917 were still months away; furthermore, the horrible face of a
new war was peering over the horizon.

I was afraid that the lesson I believed I had underlined and which
should be useful would be lost if a war was started before the
story of the mutinies was published.

So I decided to publish what I had written under the title of
Prelude to Victory, hoping that one day I would be able to write the
sequel.

But the war had barely started when the very structure of my
study showed formidable cracks. Its point had been to describe
the mutinies, talk of the disease and its symptoms, but above all to
acknowledge the debt Britain and France owed to the great doc-
tor who had devised a cure – Pétain. But by June 1940 Pétain was
the leader of the France of Vichy, which allowed herself to become involved in collaboration with an enemy bent on our destruction.

The responsibilities of the Pétain of 1917 were very different
from those he assumed in 1940, but it was the same man, however
loaded with years he had become.

Immediately after the second war ended, I simply could not
praise for his achievements the man who had so often, under the
pretext of helping France, placed weapons in Hitler's hands to use
against my country.

But the years passed, and it seemed to me to be not only a great
injustice to Marshal Pétain but a cruel distortion of history to allow
the dust of years to settle on what is, I am convinced, a heroic
achievement which in the First World War brought victory out of
defeat.

In publishing Pétain's narrative, and paying this belated tribute
to him, I dedicate this story to those magnificent soldiers, the
'*poilus*' of 1914–18.

A CRISIS OF MORALE IN THE FRENCH NATION AT WAR

16th April – 23rd October, 1917

by *GENERAL PHILIPPE PÉTAIN*
Paris, 15th May, 1926

Translated from the French
by RIVERS SCOTT

Translator's Note

General Pétain's narrative of the Mutinies, "Une Crise Morale de la Nation Française en Guerre", contains corrections to the typescript in his own handwriting. In all cases I have used the MSS version. Many passages are underlined, and these I have italicised in the English text. I have also adhered to the original in the matter of headings and sub-headings.

A Crisis of Morale
in the French Nation at War
16th April – 23rd October, 1917

Morale has always been and always will be a vital factor in the conduct of war. *Civil and military leaders must never blind themselves to its fluctuations. They must foster it by every means and, in so far as this is practicable, postpone the launching of any major operation until they have succeeded in keying it up to the highest pitch.*

This is evident enough, and one need waste no further time in enlarging on or substantiating the proposition itself. It may be interesting, however, to study one particular case, in which the ups and downs to which a nation's morale is subject can be observed in an extreme form. Such an exercise will not attempt to lay down any general laws. That could only be done if a number of situations, of widely differing sorts, were to be analysed in depth. But it may, perhaps, produce some rule-of-thumb guidance on the delicate task of handling soldiers in the mass, on what steps should be taken against a threat to an army's morale, and on the measures to be adopted to restore that morale if it has once been undermined.

Our example will be the crisis of the year 1917, when France was shaken by a short but violent revolt against the hardships of a campaign to which there seemed to be no end.

Terrible though they were, we should not hesitate to recall the events of that painful period. It is known to all the world that our tribulations were such that they brought us at last to the very edge of the abyss. At that moment, indeed, many thought we had come to the point beyond which human nature could resist no longer. Had we sunk into the abyss yawning at our feet, the nations would still have honoured us for the valour we had displayed during

three years of war. In the event, our recovery was to be the cause
of even greater rejoicing, linked as it was, and as we proudly
recall, with that of civilisation itself.

On then, and let us watch the clouds gather and the storm
break! How was it, we must ask, that this storm, as it built up,
was able to escape the attention of the most highly placed of the
country's chiefs, or, at least, that it proved too much for such
defences as they could muster against it? We shall examine
impartially whatever we may feel is susceptible of throwing
fresh light on those events, and we shall observe at close quarters
how France's tottering morale recovered and returned to con-
form to the nation's ideal. This brief review of the past will, no
doubt, give us grounds for an encouraging and hopeful outlook
on the future.

I. THE SYMPTOMS

After the glorious but gruelling ordeals of Verdun and the Somme, it would have been understandable had France decided to suspend the prodigious exertions which she had maintained for more than two years as the spearhead of the Allied war effort. Realising, however, that this was no time to relax, she initiated and took the lead at the Chantilly discussions of the 15th and 16th November 1916 when she won agreement from the rest of the Allied heads to the principle of *a general offensive on all fronts to be launched with the maximum forces available from the beginning of 1917.*

One's first response to this may be to admire greatly a resolution which seemed to indicate on the part of our leaders an indomitable will to victory and faith in its success. On reflection, one must ask oneself to what extent these leaders were prompted by a desire to make a quick end to an exhausting war at whatever immediate cost? Had they taken the pulse of the country and taken into account its state of health, would they have gone so far and so fast, at least in its application? *It is as dangerous to disregard a nation's malady as an individual's, whether the sickness is already apparent or is merely threatening;* yet this, it would seem, is just what was done in France when her leaders elected to turn a blind eye to the obvious suffering of the most important elements of the nation, that is, the non-combatants, the other ranks and the officers of the armed forces.

In the light of the well-known consequences of this omission, some interest may attach to a retrospective examination of the pathological state of the body politic in order to reveal the diagnosis that should have been made, and to analyse the means then available to the Government and to the High Command to ensure the safety and the salvation of the country.

A. THE WINTER OF 1916–17 ON THE HOME FRONT: LAUNCHING
AND EXPLOITATION OF A PACIFIST PROPAGANDA CAMPAIGN

Early stages of the campaign

On the home front confidence was clearly no longer at a level to sustain the great decisions just taken. On the contrary, doubt was spreading and, what was more serious, subversive undercurrents were being allowed to develop unchecked.

The civilian population, during the early years of the war, did not personally suffer the grim ordeal imposed by a daily attrition of body and nerves. Their spirit remained for a long time unshakeable and an optimism nourished by exaggerated newspaper articles kept them far from a sense of reality. They expected every day to hear of "The Breakthrough", and there was much cheerful talk about the devil-may-care *poilu* cracking jokes among the shell-bursts, sticking out his chest at the machine-gun bullets, and generally cocking snooks at the "Boche".

But by the end of the year 1916 this attitude of mind was a thing of the past and stark reality had shattered illusion. The public were well aware of the disastrously inadequate results of the bloody battles of the past twelve months, and, knowing that fresh waves of attacks were prepared for the coming spring, viewed with consternation the gigantic tasks that lay ahead. As enthusiasm cooled, pessimism began to take root. To many people, *victory by military means now seemed impossible.*

It was at this point that committees were clandestinely organised throughout the country and a campaign of "pacifism" was launched. The aim was to exploit the mood of discouragement setting in among the better-informed sections of the population and thereby to stir up discontent, or even open revolt and revolution, among the workers. Literature calculated to increase doubts of the justice of our cause and our chances of victory against a too powerful Germany were printed and circulated. *Meetings were organised, ostensibly for the discussion of trade union affairs, but at which syndicalist and anarchist agitators developed their subversive theories,*

promoted strikes, advocated indiscipline in the factories, a reduction in working hours, and a slowing-down of agricultural
production.

Self-interest and the ambitions of individuals took precedence
over the supreme demands of national defence on the very soil
of the invaded homeland.

And what were the authorities doing about it?

The Government turns a blind eye

Looking back at the stricken France of 1917, one must have the
courage to admit that those whose duty it was to uphold morale
were allowing the country to drift rudderless. To the cries of
alarm from the Command, what was the response from the Home
Front?

As early as the 29th December, 1916, the Commander-in-Chief
was warning the Ministry of the Interior (Security Department)
about *the circulation of anti-militarist and anarchist leaflets among the
troops.* He asked to be supplied with full details of the campaign
and its sources: lists of groups and centres of agitation and of
bookshops supplying the literature; names of known agitators
and of members of the forces in touch with them; and, generally,
all relevant information on the subject which the Security Department had succeeded in gathering.

On 5th January, 1917, the Minister of the Interior replied that
this was an impossible undertaking. He claimed that he knew
about the campaign, and was watching it closely. And he suggested that it would meet the case if a liaison officer was dispatched
to him once a week to be briefed on any new developments and
counter-measures. This amounted to a point-blank refusal to
co-operate, since it was not difficult to imagine the hopeless task
which would fall to the lot of any such wretched liaison officer
precipitated straight from the atmosphere of the front and left
stumbling around for a few brief hours in the dark and mysterious
corridors of the Security Department.

On 25th January, 1917, the Commander-in-Chief addressed an

even more desperate plea to the Minister of War. He said that *the whole front was seething with rumours of unrest in the interior, of deliberate restriction of production, of strikes in the munition-works, explosives-factories and other establishments engaged in production for the national defence.* Doubts were growing among the troops, who feared a shortage of weapons and ammunitions. *The troops themselves were becoming demoralised by the spectacle of their comrades in the factories wasting time on a succession of labour disputes in which the interests at stake appeared to be principally their own.* It was essential, the letter continued, that this most serious state of affairs should be made known to the War Cabinet and examined by them as a matter of urgency.

A month later, on 28th February, a fresh warning of these dangers was dispatched to the Minister of the Interior, with copy to the Minister of War requesting his intervention with his colleague. The rash of leaflets, the letter pointed out, was assuming the scale of an epidemic: more were now seized in a fortnight than in three months the year before. They emanated from "Libertaire", from "The Committee for the Resumption of International Relations", from "The Committee for the Defence of the Trade Union Movement", from "The Iron and Steel Federation", from "The Union of Teachers", and from the anarchist, Sebastien Faure. The agitators were in touch by correspondence with the soldiers, and included amongst the principals Sebastien Faure, Merrheim, Hubert, Benoit, Hasfeld, Brion and Mecheriakoff. A campaign of industrial and military agitation was being planned by these men, and was due to become on the 1st May a full-scale pacifist movement. The conclusion of this letter was as follows: "Action should be taken to seize the leaflets at the printing works, to ban all meetings not confined to the discussion of purely professional matters, to stop publication of the revolutionary paper *Natchalo*, to clamp down on the subversive activities of Sebastien Faure, Merrheim, Hubert, and the dozen other agitators who collaborate with them, to smash the pacifist propaganda campaign and to enforce normal working in the war factories and arsenals."

Faced with this list of categorical demands, the Minister of the Interior declined to give a direct reply, since he interpreted them as an insult and a reflection on his competence. "It appears", he wrote to the Minister of War on 3rd March, "that the purpose of this letter is to point out to me the existence of a campaign which I am assumed not to know about, or the causes of which I am thought not to have grasped. This, however, is not the case...." There followed a long statement in the course of which was set out, not the steps taken to put a stop to the campaign, but a commendation of the Security Department's prescience. He concluded by expressing the wish that there should henceforth be no direct correspondence between General Headquarters and his Ministry, and that the former would accept the decisions of his Ministry, communicated through the Ministry of War.

It is unfortunate indeed that a discussion of such importance should have been brought to a close because of one man's susceptibilities and should have failed to produce the remedies so urgently required. *It may of course be that the Ministry of the Interior, as the Minister claimed in his letter of the 3rd March, saw all that was happening and duly noted it in its files. One can only say that no evidence exists that any of the centres of agitation was ever closed down, that any of the agitators was ever arrested, or that any sort of move to suppress the campaign was made at any time.*

Extravagances of the national Press

The Press, whose role in hours of grave crisis should be to give an informed and prudent lead to public opinion, committed every sort of irresponsible folly and every sort of misjudgement and mistake. It fell into *the reprehensible habit of laying down the law about the conduct of operations.* It expressed its approval or disapproval of changes in the High Command. It printed full reports of questions and debates in Parliament. It also disclosed details of the plans drawn up, and the decisions reached, at the most highly secret conferences.

Some newspapers gave the most extensive coverage to Socialist efforts to resume international relations and to organise meetings at which party members, whether Allied, Russian, neutral, or enemy, were to discuss the prospects of peace. These newspapers played up the economic crisis, the importance of the strikes, and so on and so forth.

Such a pass did matters reach, indeed, that these mouthpieces of the nation were launching the word and the notion of "defeatism" just as the Government, whose job it was to control them, was making an all-out effort for victory.

B. EXHAUSTION AND GRIEVANCES AT THE FRONT

The criminal propaganda campaign conceived in the interior spread gradually to the front, where it found well-prepared soil. For the troops, at the end of two years of a terrible war, were physically and morally in an utterly exhausted state, and needed little urging, if encouraged, to complain of hardships which a spirit of discipline had hitherto caused them to bear in silence.

We will now consider the various grounds of these grievances, which, if dealt with in time, could no doubt have been remedied. At least they should not have been ignored when these pressures began to build up into a dangerous swell.

Irregularity of Leave

Foremost among the grievances was *the irregularity of leave and the inadequacy of leave transport arrangements*. In many units the rosters were incomplete or wrongly drawn up, and the mistakes made gave colour to complaints of injustice and unfairness. New intakes were able to get back to their families before veterans who had been far longer in the line. Officers were more favourably treated than the men. From February 1917 on, because of the imminence of the offensive, leave in the majority of units was cut down and sometimes stopped altogether. Then, when the attacks ended, it was impossible to re-establish the normal allocations in the divisions which had been engaged. Thus from the start of the mutinies the soldiers' mail is full of allusions to what the men considered to be a serious injustice: "I expect to be home before the end of the month; that is what the revolt has been about . . ." "For several days nerves in the company had been on edge; there were complaints about the unfair allocation of leave . . ." "The most serious grievance which brought this trouble about was the question of leave."

Even the lucky ones who did enjoy a reunion with their families returned with a deplorable impression of the conditions of their journey. They complained of uncomfortable trains, unprotected from the weather, always late and held up for hours in stations without shelters. They reported that there was nothing to prevent men indulging in acts of indiscipline for there were no police to be seen anywhere. The people who had it all their own way were the racketeers, who reigned supreme.

Poor food, increasing drunkenness

The soldier on leave, like the soldier at the front, marches on his stomach; and the fighting man, always hungry and always thirsty, and with a purse bulging with cash that he had no choice but to save, was an easy prey for the shoals of sharks who followed him wherever he went. He knew he was being cheated, but complained, and *he held it against the army that his basic rations were so inadequate*. What these rations were lacking in, most of all, was variety. They were often especially deficient in green vegetables. *They were badly prepared*, for the most part by "old sweats", who were chosen as cooks whatever their lack of skill or inclination. In cantonments, the dishes they served to their compulsory customers were invariably unappetising. When it was a question of getting meals up to the trenches, the distances involved and the *inadequacy of the equipment* available meant that when the food arrived it was congealed, dried up, dirty, and often absolutely disgusting.

The divisional co-operative canteens, instituted on 2nd November 1916, were not yet doing much good and could not supplement the inadequate rations. As soon as the men came out of the line and arrived in camp, they made a dive for the local shops with the intention of buying up whatever foodstuffs were offered them at whatever price, content with requiting those who fleeced them with a few oaths and finding in the experience new fuel for their resentments. The fact was, of course, that they had *too much spare cash*. Quite apart from the sums dispatched to them by their families, their advances of pay were well above what they really required. The Law of 31st March 1917 accorded special rates of pay to all those who had served two years over the legal minimum period, and a special gratuity to all who had taken part in a battle. In addition to this the Decree of 18th April 1917 guaranteed each man a share in the profit expected to be made from economies in the messing arrangements, when the cost was brought down to five francs a head. Although *half this saving was prudently set aside as a nest-egg for those entitled to it, the other half was paid over to them in cash, and this was far too much*. It was spent on whatever was available – especially wine! The craftiest dodges were used by the troops to procure alcoholic drinks, then strictly prohibited, the men being encouraged in this by many of the local inhabitants turned wine-merchants for the duration. Men would not hesitate to walk miles, where necessary, for the purpose of filling their water-bottles with *pinard*. *Drunkenness became general*, with the most deplorable effect on good order and military discipline.

Faulty organisation of rest billets

It can be stated that the misuse of the rest periods out of the line was largely due to *the discontent which the men felt at the allocation of these*, to which they felt they had a right, and which in any case they sorely needed. They felt that by misusing the rest periods when they got them they were making up in some way for the delays they had suffered.

It is undeniable that there were many units which, from Verdun and the Somme onwards, had been kept in the front line almost continuously, with no respite in which battle-shattered nerves could be restored. Other units, on the contrary, were kept in the rear for months at a time, too long not to lose their familiarity with danger and too long not to arouse bitter jealousy in the ranks of units less favoured. Here then were two abuses, at opposite ends of the scale, each involving a genuine and often serious blow to good morale. We shall illustrate their effects in a later part of this study when we show the mutiny working itself out in formations which had either had too much rest or not enough.

Another source of grievance was that the rest-quarters behind the line, usually in villages now three-quarters reduced to rubble, were totally without comfort, while the lack of any permanent staff in these places, and the rapid succession of different units in and out of them, made it impossible for them either to be looked after or kept up, or even for the billets themselves to be fairly allocated. *The best were monopolised by permanent personnel, generally belonging to rear formations.* These were not prepared to make room for newcomers except with very ill grace and were generally in league with the local inhabitants. The fighting troops were the sufferers both morally and physically from this surly treatment. They thought they deserved better.

Apparent uselessness of the sacrifices undergone

The intense suffering the combatant endured and the continuous nature of his ordeal do certainly seem to have been too often overlooked. Ever since the stabilisation of the front the war had become an obscure plodding grind, *with none of the old excitement or idealism left to relieve it*. It may be true that it called for a less violent sort of effort than did the fighting in open country. But against this it demanded inexhaustible patience, maintained under constant fire, amid mounds of rotting corpses, now in a sea of filthy mud, snow and rain, now in a desert of sun-scorched chalk, clay and sand. *This was a war of constant small engagements, of sorties of men against the barbed wire defences of well-entrenched machine-gun emplacements. The successes achieved were temporary and costly*, and the corpses left lying in No Man's Land after each one served to remind the survivors of the futility of their sacrifice. There were more important attacks, made in the hope of achieving "the break-through". But on every occasion, after a few trenches had been overrun, they foundered against carefully prepared second lines of defence, before which it became apparent that their efforts had been in vain and all was to begin again.

With such bitter disappointment as the only result of their sacrifice, *it began to be felt by the fighting troops that the High Command had no understanding of what could be done* and persisted in courses which experience had shown to be hopeless. A break-out into open country and a resumption of the "war of movement" seemed no longer possible. Confidence in a "military victory" was badly shaken. For a short time "economic victory" was canvassed instead, but this in its turn proved a source of disillusionment and no one could see any hope of ending the war.

In spite of the resounding success of our defence of Verdun and our brilliant counter-offensives at Douaumont, Vaux and the Somme, it was bitterly evident to the front-line troops that the basic position of the two sides remained unchanged. At the beginning of the third winter of the war they felt deeply the burden of their fatigue. They were nervous, impatient and restless. They grumbled. They wrote home that they wondered "if the war would ever end"; that "they were fed up"; that "the amount of ground still to be covered was appalling"; that it was not true to claim that we were stronger than the Boche; that they no longer had any idea why they were fighting; and, finally, that it was time those in command of them explained the reasons for such massacres.

Thus the fighting man whenever the opportunity offered to express his disillusionment (and the postal censorship revealed this) groused about the conduct of the war and protested against the uselessness as well as the scale of its losses and hardships. *More than this, he went on to express his conviction that the High Command had simply abandoned him to his fate, that it was totally uninterested in his welfare and morale, that it was treating him, in short, as no better than a soulless pawn.*

Defeatist attitude and lack of initiative on the part of certain officers

Faced with all this, what was the attitude of the officers? A handful responded with courage and energy. The great majority bowed before the storm and awaited events.

Practically all the old peacetime officers, who had won the respect and affection of their men and had proved their worth in the handling of their troops in action, had gone. Their replacements had had to pick up what training they could as they went along. They lacked authority to stand firm when the trouble began and to prevent its spreading by the dignity of their attitude and the force of their example. They had been faced with the same tests and experienced the same hardships as their men. They had the same private worries and were beset by the same doubts.

As for the senior officers and generals, the constant threat of being stellenbosched, inhibited and demoralised them. *Many commanders were no longer prepared to furnish their superiors with candid and full reports either about events in their sectors or the moral or material condition of their units.* To insure themselves against trouble they often descended to suppressing details capable of showing up their units in a bad light, and even to distorting the facts. Some went so far as to carry out a shameless bluff and to exploit the heroism of their men to obtain minor successes out of all proportion to the risks involved.

C. FALSE OPTIMISM AND RASHNESS IN THE DIRECTION OF THE WAR

Adoption of a strategy of boldness and risk

This obsession with rapid results, coupled with disregard of the risks involved, was for some time the characteristic attitude of the

French Command. It is here that we approach the most delicate aspect of our study, since it will be largely critical. Yet we feel it essential to speak out unambiguously if the lessons which the crisis of 1917 hold for the future are to be clearly brought out.

It is certainly true that, *at this point of the war, there was no reason to doubt that victory could be achieved so long as we confined ourselves to the possible and the practicable* – two words that were constantly on everybody's lips and should have inspired the country's leaders with a suitable programme. Unfortunately the solution decided upon to resolve the crisis in command in December 1916 and the plan of campaign which our Allies agreed to at our insistence were more than ever the product of hysterically high hopes *and of fantastic strategic over-confidence*.

The offensive fixed for the spring was planned and discussed in the full glare of publicity and presented to all as a campaign of rapid movement and far-distant objectives which was intended to force a decision. This would come, it was claimed, within forty-eight hours: the attackers would be able to sweep without difficulty or impediment through the point of rupture and beyond. . . . Such, however, was not the opinion of those who would have to carry out the plan. The mere conception of such an operation was entirely contrary to the experience acquired in two years of war at the cost of appalling sacrifices.

Weakened authority of the High Command

Graver still, *the planners were in extraordinary and strange contradiction with themselves. Having accepted the principle of a policy and a strategy based on boldness and risk, they did not hesitate to undermine the confidence which was so essential to success.* The War Council held at Compiègne on 6th April, 1917, was a real blunder, and it would have been wiser not to voice the doubts concerning the plan's success which emerged at the Conference. A ban should at least have been imposed on Press comment, to protect the prestige of those entrusted with the nation's fate. This was not done and *the whole Press of every political shade of opinion reported the doubts that had been raised* and the agonising questions which had been posed.

Relaxation of the severity of military justice

It was against this background that *the refusal to face the likelihood of a crisis in morale and to take the preventive measures the Command was clamouring for revealed itself as the official attitude.* And since the campaign for military disobedience was being allowed to develop unchecked, one may fairly ask whether any measures of repression were being taken at all.

On the outbreak of war it had been considered necessary to revise the existing legislation to enable offences against discipline to be energetically and swiftly dealt with.

The Decree of 10th August, 1914, suspended the right of appeal by convicted soldiers.

In addition to this, on 1st September, 1914, the War Minister ruled that, in capital cases, the General Officer who had authorised the indictment could confirm the sentence passed within forty-eight hours, provided he himself had not recommended to the Head of State a commutation of the sentence.

On 6th September, 1914, a new decree set up special Courts Martial to deal with men caught in the act of committing any crime coming under the Code of Military Justice (*Code de Justice militaire*) and certain crimes indictable under the ordinary *Code Pénal*. These courts consisted of three judges only; no interval was necessary between the charging of the accused and his trial; judgement could be given by a majority of two to one, and was subject neither to revision nor to appeal.

The Courts Martial were also empowered to try civilians if their case involved any crime or misdemeanour affecting public order and security.[1] And when a trial was held at the front it was not open to the court either to admit evidence of extenuating circumstances[2] or to give suspended sentences.[3]

[1] Article 8 of the Law of 9th August, 1849.
[2] Article 1 of the Law of 19th July, 1901.
[3] Article 1 of the Law of 28th June, 1904.

These provisions, although unquestionably severe, had been regarded by previous responsible governments as both necessary and just. Now they were or were about to be gradually withdrawn, despite the Commander-in-Chief's protests.

General Joffre put this view before the Government on several occasions[1] in the hope of preventing what he believed would be a harmful step, and in this connection it may be interesting to quote from one of his letters, dated 8th March, 1916:

"There are occasions when nothing but the fear of immediate punishment can stop a man committing a crime. If a soldier deserts his post, refuses to obey an order, strikes or insults a superior officer, it is essential that immediate retribution be meted out so that none of his comrades shall dare to imitate his behaviour. The example made will produce virtually no effect unless conviction and penalty follow hard on the heels of the fault. . . . The reasons which justified the taking of exceptional measures in an hour of grave crisis have not become less valid now. . . ."

The General might as well have saved his breath to cool his porridge. The desire for the introduction of lenient measures overrode reason. French generosity followed its natural and irresistible bent. The result was that the convictions by Military Courts for offences against military discipline rose from 14,479 in 1915 to 24,953 in 1916, then rocketed the following year, to a new peak figure of 37, 842.

The Law of 27th April, 1916 suppressed the special Courts Martial and re-established the admissibility of evidence of extenuating circumstances and the right to give suspended sentences. It further deprived the military courts of their right to try civilians, except for crimes and offences touching on national defence.

A Decree of 8th June, 1916, reintroduced the right of appeal against the death sentence.

On 20th April, 1917, the Minister of War, reversing the decision of his predecessor dated 1st September, 1914, relating to convictions on capital charges, forbade the General Officer who

[1] Letters from the Commander-in-Chief dated 26th September, 23rd November, 18th December, 1915, and 2nd August and 8th March, 1916.

had convened the Court to have the sentence carried out without the express authority of the Head of State.

While a desire to mitigate the harsh provisions of military justice is understandable on humanitarian grounds in normal times, it is certainly unjustified in periods of national crisis such as that through which the French nation was now passing. It may well be that certain mistakes were committed, for which those responsible should be brought to account. But this did not prove that the system as a whole was wrong; nor can it be denied that the Courts Martial administered the Code with unfailing moderation and a constant care for justice.

II. THE CRISIS

Towards the end of April 1917, the fortune of war appeared to turn against the Allied armies after having smiled on them for a brief moment. The dazzling hopes of the early spring, which the German withdrawal to the Hindenburg Line, America's entry into the war, and the anticipated impact of the Franco-British offensives had caused the leaders of the Coalition to hold out, were dashed to the ground. *The grand strategic triumph on which so much had been staked turned into a series of dearly-bought minor successes in a prolonged campaign of merciless attrition.* Russia defaulted and her army began to disintegrate. The newspapers reported, often with approval, the early revolutionary measures – the setting up of workers' and soldiers' committees, the abolition of saluting and of military ranks. The enemy Command, its confidence restored, directed with dogged determination the battles in Artois, the Chemin-des-Dames, and Champagne, and after holding up our progress, banked on renewing their successes.

The French army was exhausted. Hopelessness and *pessimism spread to it* from the interior, *swamping as it did so the mood of superficial enthusiasm, whipped up from above,* which had never really taken root.

The fighting troops were at the end of their tether. Those in authority must have seen this quite well, yet they continued to count on them, so often in the past three years had they witnessed their capacity for performing the impossible. This time, however, *there were men in the ranks who not only could not but would not answer the call. This was the crisis.* It struck, like a bolt from the blue, among the units due to be sent up the line to the two deadliest of the danger-spots, the Chemin-des-Dames and the Monts-de-Champagne.

First incidents between 29th April and 17th May. Reorganisation of the French High Command. Gravity and rapid extension of the crisis.

On 29th April an infantry regiment stationed at Mourmelon was ordered up the line to the sector of the Moronvilliers Heights, where it had carried out attacks on the 17th April and subsequent days and from which it had been withdrawn for a short period of rest only five days before. It was known to the men that they would be employed in a new offensive. They also knew that their division was being sent back into action when other major formations which had also taken part in the attack of 17th April were still resting far from the front. Two or three hundred men, almost all from the battalion chosen to lead the new offensive, failed to appear when their unit was leaving for the front and then announced that they would not march. The unit's officers and NCOs proved incapable of quelling the outbreak, which, how-ever, was put down by the divisional commander within twenty-four hours.

News of this incident soon got round and other mutinous out-breaks followed. On 4th May a number of sudden desertions occurred among members of an infantry regiment[2] in action in the Chemin-des-Dames area. In the quarters of a colonial regiment[3] due to take part in an attack in the same sector *the men noisily refused to fight*, an action clearly provoked by the circulation of leaflets on which were blazoned such inflammatory slogans as "Down with the War!", "Death to the Warmongers!", etc. On 16th and 17th May serious trouble of a similar nature broke out in a battalion of Chasseurs,[4] and in an infantry regiment[5] in a reserve position on the Aisne. These unhappy incidents multiplied to a point where *the safety and cohesion of the whole army were in jeopardy*.

It was precisely on this same date, the 17th, that the French

[1] 20th Infantry Regiment, 33rd Infantry Division.
[2] 321st Infantry Regiment, 133rd Infantry Division.
[3] 43rd Colonial Infantry Regiment of the 2nd Colonial Infantry Division.
[4] 25th Battalion of Chasseurs-à-pied, 127th Infantry Division.
[5] 32nd Infantry Regiment, 18th Infantry Division.

High Command was reorganised. Its first duty was to assess objectively the seriousness of the trouble so as to weigh the gravity of its task. It saw the deadly virus of indiscipline spreading. It received alarming reports from all sides. They poured in – almost uninterruptedly, alas!

19th May: In a Chasseur battalion[1] south of the Aisne three armed companies staged *noisy demonstrations* in cantonments.

20th May: Two complete infantry regiments[2] in the Chemin-des-Dames sector refused to obey orders. Individual *acts of insubordination* were reported in an infantry regiment[3] in the same area.

21st and 22nd May: In an infantry regiment[4] resting in the Tardenois district an attempt was made by agitators to stir up trouble among the men. *Delegates were elected to present at headquarters a protest against a continuation of the offensives;* a group of trouble-makers marched to the divisional depot and created a disturbance. Nearby, in another infantry regiment[5] in the same division, *groups of soldiers turned on their officers, sang the Internationale and threw stones at them.*

25th May: In the Vosges, up to that time completely untroubled by the outbreaks, one section of an infantry regiment[6] refused to embus for the front. They were incited to this act of defiance by their own sergeant.

26th May: Three infantry regiments[7] of a division recalled to the front after a rest period in the Aisne sent representatives to join *in discussions at which plans for an attempted general mutiny were being hatched.*

27th May: Demonstrations and disturbances occurred in an

[1] 26th Battalion of Chasseurs-à-pied, 166th Infantry Division.
[2] 128th Infantry Regiment, 3rd Infantry Division; and 66th Infantry Regiment of the 18th Infantry Division.
[3] 90th Infantry Regiment, 17th Infantry Division.
[4] 267th Infantry Regiment, 69th Infantry Division.
[5] 162nd Infantry Regiment, 69th Infantry Division.
[6] The 54th Infantry Regiment of the 12th Infantry Division.
[7] The 224th, 228th and 329th Infantry Regiments of the 158th Infantry Division.

infantry regiment[1] out of the line in Lorraine. In the Tardenois district the men of an infantry regiment[2] *shouted seditious slogans, sang the Internationale, and insulted and molested their officers while the regiment was embussing.*

28th May: *A serious extension of indiscipline and mutiny* was reported from six infantry regiments,[3] a battalion of Chasseurs, and a regiment of dragoons stationed on the Aisne and farther south.

29th, 30th and 31st May: The situation deteriorated and indiscipline spread to the majority of the regiments of eight divisions[4] and to a colonial artillery regiment,[5] all of which had been in action in the Chemin-des-Dames sector or were about to be sent back there.

1st, 2nd and 3rd June: *Zenith of the crisis.* In fifteen to twenty units belonging to sixteen divisions,[6] either in action or resting in the same area, men of all arms were involved for three days in the most violent outbreaks of disorder.

This catalogue of disturbances, shocking though it is, still gives an inadequate picture of the plight of the French army as the intoxicating madness spread. A detailed examination of some of the most typical cases will help us to understand better the anguish of the High Command under the threat of this appalling danger.

Example of a premeditated and methodically planned mutiny in a regiment: 28th – 30th May

This was an example of a type of mutiny *conceived in cold blood,*

---

[1] The 298th Infantry Regiment of the 63rd Infantry Division.
[2] The 18th Infantry Regiment of the 36th Infantry Division.
[3] The 4th, 82nd and 313th Infantry Regiments of the 9th Infantry Division; the 224th and 228th Infantry Regiments of the 158th Infantry Division; the 129th Infantry Regiment of the 5th Infantry Division; the 66th Battalion of Chasseurs-à-pied of the 9th Infantry Division; and the 25th Dragoons of the 1st Cavalry Division.
[4] Units of the 5th, 6th, 13th, 35th, 43rd, 62nd, 77th and 170th Infantry Divisions.
[5] The 3rd Regiment of Artillery of the 1st Colonial Army Corps.
[6] Units of the 5th, 6th, 13th, 24th, 28th, 41st, 46th, 47th, 62nd 64th, 70th, 71st, 77th, 81st, 170th and 177th Infantry Divisions.

systematically organised and obstinately conducted in an infantry regiment[1] which up to that moment had been regarded as quite first class. Planned over a long period, it developed without a hitch, and in an atmosphere of total assurance.

This unit had taken part in May 1916 in the first attempt to recapture Fort Douaumont, where it showed great courage and sustained heavy losses. From June 1916 to February 1917 it was almost continuously in the line in the tough Eparges sector, exposed to constant shelling, surprise attacks and enemy mines. A this point *symptoms of serious physical and moral exhaustion* became noticeable in its ranks – symptoms which affected the junior officers as well, and to which their superiors, up to the regimental and brigade commanders themselves, appeared to pay too little regard, whereas it should have made them doubly watchful and active, doubly willing to show themselves and take personal risks, to give encouragement and set an example. Action had been taken against certain of these officers whose grip on the situation had been notoriously feeble, and in February 1917 the unit was withdrawn for a rest. By the spring, there were grounds for hoping that when it returned to the fighting line it would once more justify its former reputation. But this moment was delayed, since the grand plan for a strategic exploitation of the attack of 16th April failed to materialise, and *the regiment was left in inglorious inactivity near Paris.* There the men, too closely in touch with the rear, were affected by the bad spirit in the interior. They listened to the *complaints of a multitude of camp-followers whose attitude reflected the labour unrest and strikes spreading throughout the country.* They settled down all too well to their prolonged inactivity, to the absence of danger, and to the enjoyment of the comforts which came their way as a result. And when, on Whit Sunday, the lorries arrived to bring this agreeable and restful existence to an end, and trundle them off to the dreaded destination of Laffaux, the harrowing farewells overcame their sense of duty. It was then that *they began to be influenced by the propaganda directed at them at the departure point, and to believe – what they*

[1] 129th Infantry Regiment of the 5th Infantry Division.

were always being told – that they would be fools indeed to go and get themselves killed when so many others had apparently refused to march.

On 28th May, at the end of its journey, the regiment installed itself in three small villages in a sector to the south of Soissons.

After the midday meal, '*la Soupe*,' between 150 and 180 men attended a meeting in one of the hamlets, listened to a number of inflammatory speeches, fell in on the road in marching order, and coolly informed their company officers, when these arrived to disperse them, *that they refused to go up to the line. They had*, they said, *had enough of the war. They wanted a cease-fire immediately* and thought the Deputies had been wrong in December not to negotiate on the German proposals. They claimed that as Russia crumbled, leaving the German war-machine free to re-mass on the French front, the Government were simply pulling the wool over people's eyes, and that in fact everyone knew that the Americans would not be able to come into the war in time to be of any use. The fighting soldiers, they complained, were not getting proper leave; their rations were inadequate, their wives and children were "starving to death". *They were no longer willing to sacrifice their lives when shirkers at home were earning all the money, taking the women around in cars, cornering all the best jobs, and while so many profiteers were waxing rich.*

The mood of these demonstrators was calm and resolute. They were not drunk. They wanted their protest reported to the Government. They still respected their officers and dispersed when these told them to do so.

Misled by the ease with which they appeared to have won this round, the officers, from the divisional commander down to the most junior second lieutenants, spent the night of the 28th/29th advising each other that the best line to adopt *was one of patience and accommodation.* They moved around talking to each other when each officer should instead have returned immediately to exert his authority in his unit. They looked on the mutineers, naïvely, as mere strikers whom words would certainly soon restore to a better way of thinking. Then at dawn on the 29th they all returned to their units, with instructions to put the men to light fatigues around the camp, to give them a few pep talks, but to make no reference to the outbreak of the day before, and, most important, in no circumstances to resort to force, even if individual soldiers or groups of men tried to go off on their own.

This made it possible for the demonstrators of the day before to assemble again on the morning of the 29th and form themselves into a column – this time some 400 strong. Most of these had got themselves up to look like *strikers*, and appeared with walking sticks, flowers in their button-holes, and unbuttoned jackets. They marched in turn to the quarters of each of the two other battalions. There they were joined in the course of the morning by several hundred more supporters. By the end of the midday meal there were more than 800 of them, from every unit in the regiment. They answered to a bugle, and in due course moved off to rally support from the regiment next in line. Their discipline was excellent. They had been told by their leaders to do nothing which might provoke violence and to confine themselves to signifying *their fixed and unalterable determination to take no part in any further costly attacks*. They made this point firmly to the Divisional Commander. "You have nothing to fear, we are prepared to man the trenches, we will do our duty and the Boche will not get through. But we will not take part in attacks which result in nothing but useless casualties. . . ." They maintained the same position when harangued by the Corps Commander, who upbraided them, offered them fatherly advice, and threatened dire punishments in his various attempts to move them. All to no avail. With unshakeable politeness they repeated their complaints against the Government and what was happening in the interior, adding that *they would hold the line but would refuse to take part in any new offensive and demanded immediate peace*. About midafternoon they reached the quarters of the neighbouring regiment. Here the mutineers were fewer in number but much wilder. They urged them to be calm and to maintain respect for their officers. Then, *led on as usual by some extremely skilful organisers*, who seem from the evidence to have acted like true mob leaders throughout, they decided to continue their impressive march round the other units of the division and then to go on and capture some trains in which to set off for Paris with their own crews in the drivers' cabs. But, if necessary, they were prepared to march on the capital by stages in order to bring their demands before the Chamber of Deputies. Meanwhile they returned to their own cantonments for the night.

At dawn on the 30th, under orders from the High Command, motor convoys arrived at the camps to act as transport for the three battalions. This time all the officers were at their posts, and with tougher instructions. They shouted louder than the agitators and made their men obey them. The mutineers put up some resistance but did board the lorries. On the journey they continued their attempts at incitement, and tried to stir up the troops they met on the way. They made "hands up" and "thumbs down" signs. They whistled. They sang the Internationale. They waved bits of red cloth. They distributed leaflets containing the text of their refusal to fight and encouraged others to follow their example.

On the evening of the 30th and on the following days the regiment was halted in isolation from other units, then moved to the Verdun sector by train. The rebellious spirit persisted, but the demonstrations became less frequent. The High Command split up the battalions, and during the month of June *Courts Martial were held*. A corporal and three privates were sentenced to death for "deserting their post and refusing to obey orders in the presence of the enemy". The regiment itself supplied the firing squads and several detachments for the expiatory ceremony, which took place without incident on 28th June. *On 29th June, the regiment was stripped of its colours*. The battalion to which the leading spirits of the mutiny had belonged was disbanded on 16th July, and the necessary new postings among the officers took place.

That was the end of it. In July the two remaining battalions gave an honourable account of themselves at Verdun. In 1918 the regiment was reconstituted. It was twice mentioned in dispatches, received back its colours, and was decorated with the lanyard of the Croix de Guerre on the very spot where the 1917 mutinies had taken place.

Example of a violent outbreak in a regiment of the line: 1st–3rd June

Another type of *outbreak was violent in character and the spirit animating it was revolutionary.*

Here again our example is an infantry regiment,[1] with a first-class record and reputation and forming part of a crack division. After much hard fighting during the battle of the Somme, it was not sent back to rest as it had been led to hope that it would be. Instead, it was moved to the Argonne sector, where it suffered heavy casualties during the winter of 1916–17. It took part in the April offensive, achieving an appreciable but exceedingly costly success. It was then kept for five weeks in the line, although nearly all the neighbouring units were sent back to be reconstituted. Finally, it was sent to rest in the Tardenois area and was looking forward to catching up on its arrears of leave, when, after only a few days, on the afternoon of 1st June, the order came to return to the trenches.

At 1 pm on that day, angry protest broke out in the camp. The Colonel and the other officers rushed to the scene, but their attempts to control the disorder had little or no result. At 5 pm a procession was formed and moved off to the strains of the Internationale. *The Brigade Commander, who acted with energy, was given a violently hostile reception and greeted with cries of "Kill him!" Insults were hurled at him. He was pushed and jostled. The stars on his cuffs and his epaulettes were ripped off, as was the flag on his car.* The Divisional Commander succeeded with difficulty in forcing his way to the town hall, in front of which the mutineers were assembled. He was unable to make himself heard above the shouts and was forced by threats to postpone the regiment's departure for the front. Meanwhile, *some of the mutineers had armed themselves with wire cutters and cut the barbed wire round the punishment centre.* The prisoners were released and one of them, a lawyer,

[1] 23rd Infantry Regiment of the 41st Infantry Division.

and editor of a trench newspaper, became the guiding spirit of the revolt. "Friends," he told his rescuers, "I am delighted that our movement has met with such success. We shall not be alone. I have channels of information which enable me to tell you as a fact that this evening twelve divisions have taken the same action as ourselves. Cars from Paris have set out for every sector with the mission of bringing this good news to all our comrades." The mutineers, still shouting murderous threats against their Brigadier, broke the windows and doors of the town hall with paving stones, overturned the lorries in the streets, broke the windows of houses and forced the occupants to join them.

The morning of the 2nd June began rather more calmly, though crowds of drunken soldiers were still milling about in disorderly mobs, singing the Internationale and sporting red flowers in their jackets. *The organisers of the outbreak had had numerous posters stuck up on the walls bearing the words: "Vive la Paix au nom de toute l'Armée!" ("Long live Peace, in the name of the whole Army!")* with the result that, that evening, a new mob of demonstrators, about 2,000 strong, were repeating the exploits of the evening before, *with red flags flying* and shouts of "Long live the Revolution! Down with the war! Long live Peace! Down with tyrants!"

On 3rd June and during the next few days the regiment was moved in lorries to another camp, and the trouble subsided – far more quickly than could have been hoped – as the principal trouble-makers lost their hold over the men. Very soon the agitation had died down altogether and the men had returned, without exception, to the path of duty.

Further examples of violent outbreaks among fighting units and on the trains: 2nd–8th June

Other scenes of violent mutiny. On the evening of 2nd June, in the same area, there were rumblings of unrest in the cantonment of a battalion of Chasseurs[1]. The commanding officer and a cap-

---

[1] The 70th Battalion of Chasseurs-à-pied of the 47th Infantry Division.

tain who stepped in vigorously were repulsed with stones and sticks and forced to take refuge in the CO's lodgings. *The front of the house was sprayed with bullets from the mutineers' automatic rifles*, and the Adjutant and another officer who attempted to come to the rescue of their superior officer were chased across the neighbouring gardens. *The insurgents set fire to the huts of a company which attempted to oppose the revolt, and engaged in a veritable running battle, in which several NCOs and Chasseurs were wounded.* As night ended, they retired exhausted to their huts, and no repetition of this outbreak occurred next day.

On the evening of 7th June, an incident took place at Château-Thierry station, where men *off a leave-train returning from Paris threw stones at the lamps in the entrance, sang the Internationale and shouted anti-war slogans.* A railway official, a man in his fifties, was savagely struck. A posse of policemen hurried to the scene and found themselves involved in a real battle. Their chief was wounded and had to be rushed to hospital. When an effort was made to get the train on its way, *the men jammed the brakes on, then charged onto the platforms and rushed the station manager's office* to demand the release of two of their number who had been placed under arrest. They did not return to their carriages until a company of armed troops had arrived to restore order, and then not before they had successfully demanded that the latter sheathe their bayonets. *And when the train did move, it was with the shouted threat: "We'll be back soon – with grenades!"*

The same thing happened at Esternay on 8th June. *The men of the leave draft, shouting noisily, rushed at the RTO, who attempted to arrest two of them and get them back on to their train. They beat him with sticks, punched him in the face, knocked him down, and only let him go when he was no longer physically in any condition to exert his authority.* They manhandled another officer in the outer entrance of the station. They invaded the station master's office after breaking the windows, shouted and hurled insults at the station master when he tried to interfere, then gradually dispersed and got back into the trains bound for their various destinations.

General character of the crisis from June to September

The mutinies took many forms, of which examples of the most typical have been given above, and reached their peak on 2nd June, when seventeen outbreaks were reported. The situation remained serious up to 10th June, with an average of seven incidents a day. During the rest of the month the daily average was one. In July the total fell to seven incidents altogether, in August to four, and in September to one.

Altogether, *151 incidents were recorded and examined, of which 110 were concerted outbreaks of genuine gravity.* Out of the total of 151, 112 took place in the Aisne area behind the Chemin-des-Dames sector of the front (plus five on the other parts of the front but among units which had come from the Chemin-des-Dames sector). Eight occurred in the Monts-de-Champagne district (plus two which took place in other parts of the front but involved troops from Champagne), and twenty-two occurred in various other parts of the army zone.

A total of 110 units were affected. Sixty-eight of them were present (in the line or in reserve) on the Aisne on 16th April, and six were before Monts-de-Champagne. Between them they consisted of:

76 Infantry Regiments
2 Colonial Infantry Regiments
21 Chasseur Battalions
1 Territorial Infantry Regiment
8 Artillery Regiments
1 Regiment of Dragoons
1 Senegalese Battalion

These units belonged to fifty-four different divisions – that is, more than half the total number of divisions in the French army at that time.

Disturbances also occurred on 110 trains and had repercussions in 130 stations due to repeated acts of indiscipline along the whole length of the lines. These disorders were an extension of those in the interior of the country, and all converged to reach their point of greatest intensity in the areas just behind the line. Angoulême, Bordeaux,

Nantes, Toulouse, St Pierre-des-Corps, St Etienne and Limoges had all been centres of serious unrest. This spread along the lines of communication towards the army zone until it reached the main lines, of which the principal was the line Paris – Châlons – Nancy.

Such was the storm of madness which for several weeks swept a harassed and distracted France, threatening to blind her both to her objectives and to her duties.

III. THE REMEDIES

Since it was they who had allowed this evil to well up and reach the proportions of a flood, it was now the responsibility of the civil power to cut it off at its source and to make good the damage which it had caused to the national interest. While still reeling from the shock of their disillusion in the spring of 1917, they appeared determined not to fail in this task, the difficulty as well as the importance of which they fully recognised. Having re-organised the High Command of the armies, they gave it their full confidence. It was for the High Command to take the necessary steps to restore the balance of our fortunes in face of the enemy. It was the responsibility of the Government to supply it with the means it required, and to give it unfailing support; and this it promised to do.

The High Command lost no time in setting to work. It had a clear understanding of the causes of the crisis, and was determined to tackle them one after the other in whatever order circumstances might dictate.

The aims of its immediate measures were as follows:

To reaffirm the authority of military law and to secure the immediate arrest of the principal trouble-makers;
To stiffen the morale of the officers and to lay down a line of conduct which they must follow in order to regain the confidence of their men;
To protect the armies against contamination from the interior;
To draw up a new set of operational directives in conformity with what could actually be achieved.

Then would follow longer-term measures to be applied systematically to cure the disease and prevent its recurrence.

These would be as follows:

With regard to the morale of the troops, no pains would be spared in providing for the welfare of the men who were bearing so much, in keeping them contented and raising their spirits by a fair allocation of military honours and leave, by improving the rations, combating drunkenness, and encouraging saving; and also, finally, by the efficient supervision of rest arrangements and rest camps;

In general, the spirit prevailing in the country at large and the lead to be given to the national Press would both continue to be closely studied;

On the tactical level, efficient training would be reintroduced, so that the troops engaged in future operations could look forward to achieving greater successes with fewer losses and would be given fresh confidence that they possessed the means to win.

It may be of interest to take the items of this list in order, and to study how the High Command's measures made themselves felt and the support afforded it by the Government.

A. IMMEDIATE MEASURES

Re-establishment of the authority of military law and action taken against the guilty

In the grave circumstances of the moment, the most urgent necessity was that the activity of the principal trouble-makers should be broken on the spot. *Mutineers, drunk with slogans and alcohol, must be forced back to their obedience, and every means must be used to reduce to impotence the criminals who had exploited the distress of the fighting troops.*

The Commander-in-Chief, from the moment he took up his post, directed all his activities to this end, and, first by word of mouth, in the course of his tours of inspection, and afterwards in his written orders, demanded an attitude of inflexible firmness.

One of the most forcefully worded of his directives was that of 8th June: "At the time of the recent incidents, certain commanders do not appear to have done their duty. Some officers concealed from their superiors the signs of a spirit of unrest in their regiments. Others failed to tackle the trouble with the necessary initiative and energy. It is essential that officers should understand fully the responsibility they bear in such a situation. Inactivity here is equivalent to complicity. The Commander-in-Chief will mete out appropriate punishment to all who have shown weakness. He will, by contrast, uphold with his authority all those who display vigour and energy in suppressing the disturbances. . . . Certain officers or NCOs, as an excuse for not doing their duty, claim that since the outbreaks are collective in character it is difficult for them to single out the leaders. This argument is unacceptable. It is, in fact, always possible to turn collective disobedience into disobedience by individuals. All that is necessary is to tell certain men, starting with the most disaffected, to carry out some order. If they refuse, such men are at once arrested and handed over to the law, which should take its course as swiftly as possible."

In the spirit of this directive, the penalties imposed were severe. *The first to feel their force were the commanders of all units who had shown weakness incompatible with their duty and had failed to react after the first moment of surprise.* Two generals, nine lieutenant-colonels, fourteen battalion commanders and eighteen lieutenants or second lieutenants were deprived of their commands, being either relegated to less important posts, stripped of their temporary ranks, or posted elsewhere.

At the same time, on its own initiative or by goading the Government into action, the High Command worked to *re-establish most of the measures for suppressing indiscipline in the armies which had been gradually whittled away in 1916 and 1917.*

On 1st June, with the Government's authorisation, it ruled that, *wherever the gravity of the crime demanded prompt and exemplary punishment, an accused man should be brought straight before a Court Martial, without the benefit of preliminary proceedings,* and that proof of guilt supplied by direct examination of the accused should be deemed to be sufficient. In a capital case, once the sentence had been confirmed, either through the failure of the accused to lodge an appeal within the limits of the time allowed by law, or because his appeal had been rejected, it was laid down that the formation to which the Court Martial was responsible should telegraph to GHQ stating its reasons for demanding immediate execution of sentence; and that this sentence should be carried out as soon as the Commander-in-Chief had telegraphed giving the agreement of the Head of State.

On 8th June a Presidential Decree *limited the right of appeal against the death sentence*. Traitors convicted of inciting and aiding troops to go over to the enemy or join an armed rebellion were deprived of the right of appeal, as were the instigators or leaders of mutinies who had committed acts of violence during armed disturbances, refused to disperse or persisted in their indiscipline.

On 11th June the Minister of War notified the Commander-in-Chief that the *military authority would no longer be required to submit the transcript of a capital trial to the President of the Republic, if the requirements of discipline and national defence absolutely demanded that a sentence be carried out without delay* and if the sentence in question was for concerted or collective crimes, inciting men to go over to the enemy or join in an armed rebellion, dereliction of duty, usurpation of authority, or, finally, the commission of any destructive act endangering defence, the supply of provisions, or munitions of war. In any of these cases, *sentence of death would be carried out as soon as the authorisation of the Commander-in-Chief had been requested and obtained by telegram*. It was necessary, however, that the request should indicate how the votes of the Court Martial had been cast, which articles of the Code were cited in the indictment and whether one or more of the judges had been in favour of granting leave to appeal or had made a recommendation for mercy. In this way the possibility of swift action was guaranteed, while at the same time care was taken to leave intact certain safeguards for the benefit of any man who had had the misfortune – or would in future have the misfortune – to expose himself to the consequences of his own act of criminal folly.

The exceptional measures agreed to by the Civil Power for the emergency were only conceded for a short period. *On the 14th July they were revoked and the milder legislation introduced in 1916 and 1917 was revived.* The emergency measures were, however, in force long enough to enable the most urgent measures of repression to be taken and to bring the crisis under control.

Altogether, between May and October, 412 men were condemned to death by the Courts Martial, 203 of whom were sentenced in June, 386 for offences against military law or for acts of rebellion and twenty-six for common law offences. In consequence of the large number of free pardons and commuted sentences, *only seven men were, in fact, executed immediately, by order of the Commander-in-Chief, and only forty-eight after the Head of State had confirmed the sentence.*[1]

The stern penalties imposed on the self-confessed leaders of the mutiny, on trouble-makers and those convicted of serious acts of violence, had a deterrent effect which was all the more striking in that they followed so swiftly on the heels of the crimes themselves. They were also enough, though comparatively few in number, to put a stop to the dangerous activities of the agents of revolutionary propaganda.

In a note to the armies dated 10th June the Commander-in-Chief drew the attention of senior Commanders to the necessity *not to give suspended sentences except in the case of convicted men whose conduct and record had been such as to justify the belief that they would not continue to be trouble-makers in their units.* The Commander-in-Chief gave this warning because of the number of cases in which Courts Martial had given only lenient sentences to mutineers. He went on to state that it might even be necessary to revoke the suspension of sentences in the case of convicted men whose attitude and bad example undermined discipline. This would make it possible to remove from their units (deciding each case on its merits so that the manner of their removal did not serve merely to spark off further trouble) men of a specially corrupted or

[1] Of these fifty-five executions, only thirty were concerned with the re-establishment of morale.

dangerous sort whose conviction had been for crimes against the common law or for such misdemeanours as assault and battery, offences against public decency, robbery, fraud, false pretences, subversion of morals, procuring, rebellion, acts of violence against the agents of constituted authority, black-market deals in food, vagrancy, begging, and incitement to desertion and disobedience.

Finally, in the exceptional cases where the punishment and weeding out of individuals proved ineffective, it was necessary to resort to the weapon of collective sanctions. We have mentioned one such case, where a regiment was deprived of its flag and a battalion which was found to be seriously corrupted by the spirit of rebellion was disbanded. Happily, such cases were exceedingly rare and the deprivations invariably temporary, since the units affected all recovered a healthy spirit within a very short time.

By 18th June the Commander-in-Chief was already able to inform the Minister of War that, so far as discipline at the front was concerned, severity could from now on be gradually relaxed: "I began by taking immediate steps to put down all acts of serious indiscipline. . . . I shall continue this policy, never forgetting, however, that it is being applied to soldiers who have spent three years with us in the trenches and are 'our soldiers'."

Measures to restore a proper spirit among the officers and confidence among the men

To influence the healthy elements in the army and to restore the lost confidence of the officers, the Commander-in-Chief published a Note on 19th May. This read:

"I consider it time to draw the attention of all officers to the importance of maintaining high morale in the commissioned ranks.

"Officers who have displayed heroic courage for almost three years hesitate to inform their superior officers of the difficulties they face in carrying out their duties, for fear of being taxed with faint-heartedness.

"The result of this timid reluctance to speak out is that senior commanders persist with plans which would unquestionably have been altered or postponed had they been better informed. Often, preparations for an attack have been made in the absence of such necessary information.

"It is up to commanding officers to adopt an attitude which will abolish this tendency.

"A superior officer, in his relations with his subordinates, must at all times show himself approachable and friendly, willing to help them in finding solutions to the difficulties that hamper their work, ready to pass on any useful information and even to invite it.

"In present-day conditions of warfare the murderous fire-power of modern weapons means that nothing can be left to chance. Planning for even the smallest operation must be undertaken in the minutest detail, and demands the co-operation and goodwill of all concerned.

"Once, however, the preparations are complete, the decisions made and the orders given, the operation must be carried through with a vigour and determination which holds nothing back.

"An attitude of kindliness and goodwill on the part of commanders is in the noblest tradition of the French army and in no way excludes firmness.

"It is when such an attitude is lacking in a unit that an unfortunate and blameworthy spirit tends to arise. Men with a chip on their shoulder confide their bitterness to the don't-cares and the incompetents, and a discontented, restless and potentially dangerous mood is gradually built up.

"The proper person to receive an officer's confidence is his chief. The chief must justify the confidence reposed in him – a confidence founded on mutual respect and on a common love of country.

"I regard it as a matter of first importance that all relationships between officers should be guided by these principles."

At every level, immediate efforts were made to spread these

ideas by word of mouth, using the medium of frequent, informal chats, unconstrained by considerations of rank. *The Commander-in-Chief himself took the lead in this, visiting a different unit at the front every day.* After inspecting it, he would gather around him the officers, NCOs, and a number of other ranks, talk to them frankly and as man to man, inviting them to forget about his rank for a few moments and to speak to him openly in their turn. He would give them his views on the general situation, speaking of the *confidence in victory* which their Allies possessed, until his listeners really felt it for themselves, and painting a picture of innumerable American troopships looming up on the horizon and making for the coasts of France. He brought within the compass of each man's understanding the basic aims of his *strategy* and how he intended to change the character of operations in order to make them less costly to our own troops and more deadly to those of the enemy. Then he would pass on, with an abrupt change of tone, to show how he intended his orders to be carried out. Turning to address the officers in particular, he would emphasise their duties and responsibilities, mercilessly castigating any failures in command but encouraging by his advice and citing as examples those who had shown firmness and courage.

Finally, he concluded these talks by giving *tangible tokens of his goodwill to the fighting men.* He distributed the *Croix de Guerre,* the Military Medal and the Cross of the Legion of Honour lavishly to all those he wished to distinguish, calling them out from the ranks and decorating them on the spot without further formalities or citations. He also distributed souvenirs, small gifts of practical value, tobacco, and so forth. Then he would tour the camp, telling the local CO to make this or that improvement. He inspected the kitchens, to make sure that the food was adequate in quality as well as quantity to satisfy the men's needs. He checked the leave rosters. In fact, in every one of these matters, he endeavoured to spur the officers on to greater efficiency while at the same time taking care not to degrade them in the eyes of their men by the way he put his questions or made his comments.

The officers, inspired by this example, acquired a better understanding of the importance of the part assigned to them and re-captured an enthusiasm which many of them had lost. *The officers, at all levels from the generals and the staff down, now looked after the men's needs and took care not to send them into action without insuring that they had adequate support and that when they withdrew from the line to rest camps both their rations and their billets were as good as they could be.* The NCOs, in the fulfilment of their duties, were once more able to look to their officers for the backing which had too often failed them when the discouragement was at its height. Given this sort of support and direction, they re-covered *a taste for acting on their own initiative* and tried once more to work with their superiors as useful members of the team.

There was a danger that the Commander-in-Chief's campaign of explanation and encouragement, primarily directed at the officers and NCOs, might take too long to make its effect felt on the rank and file. They would no doubt in time come to appreciate its results but not the reasons which had inspired it. It was essential that the private soldier should grasp this, for it was on such an understanding by the whole army that the achieve-ment of a unified effort depended. Accordingly, the Commander-in-Chief made a direct appeal to the good sense and intelligence of every soldier, in a lengthy document, summarising the main matters dealt with in his talks, and strongly emphasising *the hope of a French victory*, which was published by his orders in the army "Bulletin" in early June.

Protection of the armies against contamination from the interior

This restoration of confidence would only bear fruit if means were found to *protect the combatants from the effect of propaganda from the interior*.

As trouble spread from unit to unit, a strict watch was organised on doubtful elements in the army and an attempt made to extend this surveillance to cover the whole country. Telegraphic warn-ings were issued by GHQ to all formations concerned, naming suspects on whom the Special Service had information and giving details of their positions. The actions, contacts and correspondence of these men were watched with care, in an effort to prevent them from launching or continuing their work of pacifist propaganda and from passing on orders from organisers at home. For without question the danger came chiefly from the rear, and *the Commander-in-Chief considered it essential that the Government should launch an action parallel to his own to extirpate on the home front known centres of infection*. On the 22nd, 25th, 29th and 30th May and on 2nd June he informed the Minister that leaflets protesting against the continuation of the war had been distributed in large quantities to men on leave so that they could be distributed in the trenches and stuck up in stations and billets. Their texts constituted a whole programme of subversion. "Enough have died: Peace . . . Our womenfolk claim peace and their rights . . . etc. . . . etc. . . . ." They were printed by the "Unions of Building Workers and Navvies" and distributed by "The Committee for the Defence of the Trade Union Movement" and "The Committee for the Resumption of International Relations", which had its headquarters in Paris, at 33 rue Grange-aux-Belles. The most energetic measures were urgently needed, the Commander-in-Chief declared, "to suppress this intolerable propaganda at its source and the most energetic measures must be taken to this end".

The last of the letters cited above, that of June 2nd, listed *the steps which the Government must take:*

(a) It should control and discipline the home-front organisations whose aim was to stir up disturbances in the army and cause it to revolt and mutiny; expel suspected neutrals; imprison the nationals of enemy powers who were still moving freely about the country; and arrest all agitators and bring them to trial.

(b) Exercise censorship and direction of the Press; forbid it to criticise the High Command, the shortages of equipment, the system of allocating periods of leave and rest; see that more discretion was exercised in reporting the Russian revolution, strikes in France and peace propaganda; and emphasise the great advantage to be expected from the intervention of the United States.

(c) Hasten the review of capital sentences by the Head of State.

(d) The gangs of condemned prisoners, the companies of Bulgarian and native labourers, all of them centres of indiscipline and demoralisation, must be sent to southern Algeria and Tunisia.

Anticipating the Government's decisions, the Commander-in-Chief took it on himself to send a telegram on 27th May putting Paris out of bounds to all men on leave from the African battalions, the Foreign Legion and other special formations too easily led astray and liable by their mere presence to aggravate any unrest either in the city itself or on the trains. As regards other formations, he ordered leave in Paris to be restricted to those who would be staying there in their own homes. He made all necessary provisions so that men without families or unable to reach them who had formerly been put up in the capital itself by various welfare organisations should be offered similar hospitality in the provinces by the same organisations or their equivalents on the spot, by local families, or by farmers prepared to bring home with them comrades in the same walk of life.

At all his interviews with members of the Government, whose measures he considered both too feeble and too slow, the Commander-in-Chief never ceased to call for *speed in closing down dangerous committees and groups of trouble-makers, in particular to prohibit trades union activities by mobilised men, which were illegal, and intolerable from the disciplinary point of view, and for the banning in the interior of all meetings not held for strictly professional purposes.* In his interviews with Ministers he insisted that however repugnant such measures might be to politicians profoundly attached to democratic principles and the defence of freedom, they were none the less essential at this critical hour, when the task was to save democracy itself from enslavement, which would certainly ensue if the weakness of the French nation continued and grew worse!

His activities were dictated by the fact that he was face to face with one of the worst dangers ever to threaten a Commander-in-Chief, and by his need to see remedies like those he had applied in the army adopted throughout the country, and that without delay. He reminded the Ministers directly concerned of their responsibility for giving an impetus to the war effort and supplying what was lacking in the organisation of our armed forces. It was impossible and wrong that they should allow themselves to be swayed by the inopportune impatience of public opinion. *Their duty was clear: to wrest power from the hands of the international agitators and fomenters of revolution who, by weakening the morale of the soldiers at the front, were doing the enemy's work for him.*

Return to a realistic strategy

Finally the Commander-in-Chief considered it most urgent to prescribe the scope of future operations which would follow the disastrously ineffective spring offensives. It was with this objective that he issued his Directive No. 1 of 19th May: "The balance of opposing forces on the northern and north-eastern fronts", he wrote, "means that a break-through followed by strategic exploitation is not at present a practical possibility. For the moment, therefore, we must apply our efforts to wearing down the enemy with the minimum of losses to ourselves."

But how, in battles which always ended in stalemate, was it possible to spare our own forces while inflicting heavy losses on the enemy? In the first place, *no large-scale attacks in depth would be undertaken* until adequate manpower and material were available. Such attacks require an excessive amount of preparation, spread the effect of the artillery bombardment over too wide a target area, and thus expose the attacker to coming up against undamaged defensive positions held by an enemy who has not been taken by surprise. They are also costly in men's lives, for in such unfavourable conditions the attacking troops suffer heavier casualties than the defenders.

Instead, there would be a series of thrusts, limited in depth so as never to push our men into a salient within the reach of the enemy's reserves and exposed to his flanking fire. These thrusts would be launched in rapid succession against many different points of the front, using the element of surprise to catch the enemy at a disadvantage and taking care throughout to keep down the losses of the infantry and give them the backing of other arms.

In commenting briefly on this Directive, which formed the basis of the new strategy, it must be pointed out that, contrary to what has often been said, its key idea was not to restrict the range of attacks to a few limited objectives, but to open the way for a large number of thrusts along the whole extent of the front, each one capable of being rapidly launched, with the advantage of surprise and with a superiority of means. By mobility and an intelligent use of the resources available, we intended to shake the walls of the enemy's defence at as many different points as possible, wearing out the patience of his High Command and the fighting capacities of his reserves, while refusing ourselves to undertake any major attack until the moral, material and physical exhaustion of the enemy had reduced him to a condition of obvious inferiority.

In short, the aim was to obtain from a flexible strategy results hitherto sought from the tactical engagement of the troops. In modern warfare, even more than in that of the past, *much bloodshed can be avoided where several battles are skilfully and systematically directed in combination rather than where everything is staked on the hazard of one brutal and murderous attempted breakthrough, developed at length and with blind obstinacy at a single point.* With their limited but soundly-based experience in matters of warfare, the soldiers of 1917 understood this very well. They enthusiastically welcomed these operational reforms, and from the moment they felt the first practical effects of Directive No. 1 their morale rose strikingly.

B. LONG-TERM MEASURES

Reform of the system of incentives to good conduct: awards and leave

While giving priority to the most urgent matters, the Commander-in-Chief also took immediate steps to encourage the men and sustain them in the efforts required of them by initiating a whole series of long-term reforms. Most valuable of these in his eyes was the institution of *a fair system of awards to units and individuals*. Between May and October he persuaded the Minister to authorise the award of the lanyard of the *Médaille Militaire* to units which had received four mentions in despatches, and the lanyard of the *Légion d'Honneur* to those which had received six. To give the citations themselves more prestige, he decided in September to announce them publicly to all the local authorities – county councils, town councils, parish councils and the rest – in the places of origin and in the garrison towns of the units so honoured. Their own folk were thus given the opportunity to appreciate the valiant conduct of units drawn from their midst; and the soldiers themselves were encouraged by the feeling that at home their courage was known and applauded. Finally, in December, a decision was announced whereby all those mentioned in Army Orders would receive a diploma signed personally by the Commander-in-Chief.

The introduction of *fairer arrangements regarding leave* completed these measures of rewarding good conduct. By an order of 2nd June all troops irrespective of rank were guaranteed seven days' leave every four months, with provision, as necessary, for making up any backlog and reconstituting the rosters which in many units had been disrupted by the recent operations. On 6th September came a Ministerial note codifying the Commander-in-Chief's various regulations and enactments, and, in agreement with him, extending the three-monthly leave period from seven days to ten. In circulating these regulations in their final form to the Army, the Commander-in-Chief once more recommended units to issue passes on a "percentage" basis, as generously as they could at any given time, so as to reconcile the men's entitlement to leave with operational necessities.

Great efforts were also made *to improve the transport situation*, so that the leave drafts, particularly on their return to the front, should be able to travel *in some degree of order and comfort*. This was the theme of a number of Notes issued in May and June and summarised in an Instruction of 8th July.

The principal marshalling yards were to be equipped with the following:

– A reception centre for men going on or returning from leave;
– Railway transport and movement offices;
– A leave camp equipped with shelters and with the following facilities: time-table notice boards, telegraph offices and letter-boxes, a canteen, a military co-operative, food and wine counters, tobacco and newspaper kiosks, dining halls, wash basins and showers, latrines, recreation rooms, clocking-out gates; in addition, a free canteen run by voluntary organisations should be attached whenever possible.
– A camp for the permanent staff, complete with sick bay and visiting room, delousing and disinfection centres, police station and cells, offices and various amenities for the staff, equipment stores, and so forth.

Within a very short time a considerable number of these improvised stations had come into being. Around and alongside them *real villages sprang up, little clusters of wooden buildings gaily painted in bright colours, where the soldier on leave was welcomed when he left his train and where, as well as obtaining any information he might need, he was able to enjoy a rest that really did him good.* Women of the voluntary organisations – the Society for helping wounded soldiers, the YMCA, the '*Goutte de café*' – lavished on the men their inexhaustible fund of devotion and generosity, so that the soldier returning to his unit after a spell of leave at home was plunged back into the hard conditions of the front with less shattering abruptness than before. This humane cushioning process was much appreciated by the men, who had never resigned themselves to being treated as mere cyphers.

Besides being made much less unpleasant by these improvements, the waiting-periods at the stations were reduced to a minimum by *a better organisation of the train schedules themselves.* On 7th June the Commander-in-Chief asked the Under Secretary of State in whose province these matters fell to bring together representatives of the railways, from the interior and the army networks, *to work out revised schedules of halts at the marshalling yards and to organise more and speedier trains*. This was done to his satisfaction. On 16th June he ordered the armies to *stagger departures of leave drafts so as to regulate numbers according to the seats available on each train*. On 1st July he organised *road transport to take the men from their billets to the stations*. On 21st July he organised "assembly points" and information services at the junctions and marshalling yards so that men who were travelling on their own or had got lost could be directed to the sectors where their units were stationed. On 23rd July he issued a Note setting out in detail the duties of commanding officers and RTOs. Next he had copies of the '*Guidebook for the Use of Those Going on Leave*'[1] distributed to all the men, to supply them with information on routes and railway time-tables.

In short, a normal leave system was now able to function, and although to operate it involved great difficulties, the High Command was able to reap the benefit of having reformed it. This question of leave properly organised was perhaps the most powerful means it possessed for maintaining morale at a high level among the troops. The men on leave were released from the strict discipline of their units, but not from the framework of an orderly and disciplined routine. The police at the stations and the trains met with no trouble, and maintained authority all the more easily in that everything on the journey served to remind the men of the High Command's constant attention to their welfare.

Improvements in the rations; the fight against drunkenness; incentives to saving.

The same care was also apparent, as we shall now show, in the improvements which the High Command was anxious to make in the material conditions at the front, to the hardships of which the soldier was now returning.

[1] This Guide was originally distributed free and to begin with had no success. The men only started to make use of it when they had to pay for it.

In the first place, rations. As a result of living continuously in the open, of hard physical exertion and insufficient sleep, the troops, as is well known, developed prodigious appetites; and we have seen that during the disturbances of the spring there were frequent complaints about the inadequacy of the rations, both in quantity and quality. The Commander-in-Chief intervened frequently to remedy this. On 2nd June he urged commanding officers to pay personal attention to the *training of cooks*, and when their unit was in billets to provide them with the means of preparing more elaborate dishes than would be possible from travelling kitchens. On 12th June he ruled that in company commanders' courses a predominant place should be given to *teaching the practical aspects of catering*, and that the officers should receive instruction in such subjects as what rations their men were entitled to, the quality, preparation and serving up of foodstuffs, and the preparation of mess accounts. On 8th June he wrote urgently to the Minister of Food, telling him of the inadequate supplies of green vegetables sent to the front and demanding the regular dispatch to the army of 100 lorry-loads a day, even if this meant severely rationing those at home.

In a detailed Note of 2nd July he reminded junior officers that "it is by paying personal attention to these details, trifling though they may appear, that they will win a deep and lasting influence over their men and will be amply repaid for their trouble when the time comes to lead them in action". They were told that they must contrive to have soup, meat and vegetables served at each main meal, and that breakfast must also be organised as a light meal, consisting of coffee, soup, cold meat, pâté, sausage, sardines or cheese, according to what was available, and that they must do their best to see that food was cooked as near the lines as possible, so that the men should be able to eat it hot, or at worst still warm.

All through the second half of 1917, notably on 23rd July, 5th August and 8th and 20th November, further letters streamed into the Ministry of Food about ensuring *the regular flow of supplies and the need to reorganise the great provision centres of the interior* so as to "free them from delays and the complications of red tape and accountancy".

To improve the organisation of the "co-operatives", those indispensable means of supplying the ever-hungry soldier with a supplement to his normal rations, the Under Secretary of State at the Ministry of Supply was asked on 9th October to set up a central supply depot for the army. This proposal was immediately agreed to in principle. The depots were formed and their functions precisely defined in an Instruction of 24th November. Since they were allowed to deal with the trade and to buy in bulk, the depots were able to supply the divisional co-operatives on exceptionally favourable terms. The latter set up branches nearer and nearer the front line. From day to day, therefore, and almost immediately behind their trenches, the soldiers were able to purchase a wide variety of foodstuffs and other items at the lowest possible price, and thus, when they arrived at the rear for a rest, they did so with the extreme edge of their hunger already blunted and no longer felt impelled to blue all their money in the first few hours as they had done in the past, to the great detriment of their discipline and health.

The supply of regular and reasonable amounts of wine was another way of fighting the greatest of all dangers resulting from this appetite, that of drunkenness. Thus on 1st June the Commander-in-Chief gave orders that, when the supplies of wine sent up from the rear for sale to the troops in the army zone were in excess of the amounts required, these should be requisitioned. This prevented the retailers, professional or amateur, from encouraging the troops to drink too much, and the wine requisitioned could be used for the normal ration, which, by the terms of a Note of 8th November, was set at a litre per man per day.

Another way of protecting the soldier from the indulgence of his excessive appetites was by *encouraging him to save*. Half the men's pay, including their battle zone gratuity and share in the profit of mess economies, was advanced to them in cash, as has already been explained, the other half being put aside to form a nest-egg on demobilisation. The amount made immediately available to them was, however, still too large, considering the limited chances they had of spending it while in the line and the danger of its being simply squandered when they reached a rest area. On 7th June the Commander-in-Chief demanded the right, which was granted him by a Decree of 14th June, to have the men's savings accounts, when circumstances called for it, credited with the whole of their share of the profits accruing from econo-mies made in the mess, and also the right to raise the ceiling of those profits from five francs a head to ten, thus halving the amount the men could spend. That done, he started discussions with the Minister about a savings book for the use of men on leave in which stamps could be affixed representing the value of half their special rates of pay and battle gratuities, such sums to be cashable only at the bank or post office where the leave was to be spent. However, this reform could only be put through by legislation, and nothing had come of it by the end of 1917.

Reorganisation of rest periods

The High Command was concerned not only with *ensuring that rest periods did the men the maximum good, in restoring and consolida-ting both their physical health and their morale;* it also wished to see them *more rationally administered.*

The essentials were laid down in an Instruction of 2nd June. So far as operational necessities allowed, *units were to take turns in the line and at the rear, so that each in succession might have the benefit of a month's rest – not more, or they might grow too unused to the sense of danger.* Released from the immediate strain of the fighting and installed as comfortably as possible, they would be left to relax completely for two or three days, then launched on a course of progressive retraining which would keep them up to the mark and well occupied without exhausting them.

Directive No. 3 of 4th July, which completed the strategic re-forms begun in Directive No. 1, returned to this question of the organisation of rest periods when it dealt with the employment and quartering of reserves. It advised army group commanders to *give their major formations equal periods in and out of the line, and to arrange things in such a way as to ensure that the rest periods were never of less than a fortnight's duration.*

As can be seen by comparing these different Instructions, the rest periods were to vary between a minimum of a fortnight and a maximum of a month. A Note of 6th August laid down in detail the conditions to be guaranteed, so far as circumstances allowed, when troops were stationed in "rest zones", "transit zones", "advanced zones", or "army reserve zones". The "rest zones" were to be fully equipped with all the amenities and facilities of a proper barracks (individual sleeping quarters, permanent kitchens, water points, latrines, wash basin, showers, wash houses, drying rooms, ovens, incinerators, and so forth).

On 3rd August an emergency demand for 400,000 beds was sent to the Minister. In addition, on 9th August, the rear section of GHQ set up a factory which turned out 5,000 beds a day. On 27th September the order went out that the major formations stationed in rest areas were themselves to give a hand in the preparation of these zones by putting their engineers and territorial units at the disposal of the "zone majors" and "camp majors". Lastly, on 22nd November, orders were given to lay in stocks of bedding-straw and fuel, and to get out information leaflets to enable the troops to discover what amenities were available in their rest camps as soon as they arrived in them.

The Commander-in-Chief completed his work by encouraging sport and entertainments such as army theatricals, which refreshed the men physically and allowed them to relax their minds. Unit commanders were able to offer "prizes" which the Commander-in-Chief had procured for them in cash or in kind from many groups of businessmen and other generous donors, official or private.

Let no one be surprised at this attempt to alternate the horrors of war with the relaxation of light-hearted amusements! It was truly what was required by both the minds and bodies of these men, who, if they were not to crack under the strain of their ordeal, needed from time to time to be able to blot out completely the painful vision of the terrible drama in which they had now played their parts for almost three whole years.

General supervision of the country's morale

Despite all these precautions, the armies would still be exposed to contamination from the interior if a strict watch was not continually kept on the rear. There the convalescence would be even longer than at the front, and unless they were kept up to the mark the authorities would soon be nodding off to sleep on top of a volcano they wrongly thought to be now extinct. We will therefore add a few words in explanation of all the letters exchanged, the discussions held, and the decisions taken on the subject of keeping an over-all watch on affairs at home.

On 23rd June the Commander-in-Chief wrote to the Minister of the Interior to inform him of a serious recurrence of the pamphlet propaganda campaign: "Enough have died: Peace!" . . . "The Russian Revolution and what Socialists should be doing about it" . . . "Spreading the Gospel" . . . "A Call to the People of Paris: Peace without Annexations!" . . . "Down with the War" . . . etc. . . etc. "The Committee for the Resumption of International Relations and the Committee for the Defence of the Trade Union Movement", the Commander-in-Chief concluded, "seem to me to be playing a particularly harmful role. I call upon you urgently to take the necessary steps to suppress this renewed agitation."

On 9th July he asked the Minister of the Interior and the Minister of War *to see that he was supplied with regular information about subversive activities in the interior, so that he would be able to take steps to prevent them spreading among the troops or at least to counter their effects without delay.* In letters of 12th and 23rd July the two Ministers replied that they agreed to this request in principle.

In practice, the information supplied to the Commander-in-Chief was both spasmodic and incomplete, and he complained about this to the Minister of War on 28th July: "I am thus left in total ignorance of the present direction of the pacifist propaganda campaign and of the demonstrations in support of it. . . . I remain powerless against its machinations. . . . I ask you to put pressure on the Minister of the Interior to have the exchange of information about the pacifist campaign between the Security Department and my Intelligence Branch resumed. . . . When winter starts, the knowledge that the campaign is going to drag on must be expected to produce a feeling of weariness among the troops, and we must take steps to prevent the pacifist organisations from taking advantage of this temporary mood as they did before. . . ."

The clash between the Commander-in-Chief and the Minister of the Interior, which occurred for a short time in the days which followed the disturbances and was concerned with the steps needed to prevent their return, sprang from the difference between the two men's points of view. Both, no doubt, were equally concerned for the safety of the country, but the one had seen the danger at less close range than had the other, had not measured its full importance, and had bowed once more *to the Frenchman's unshakeable habit of putting respect for the liberty of the individual above all else, of wanting to let bygones be bygones and show mercy to those who had failed.* But the hour when such an attitude could be countenanced had not yet struck, and those at the front were determined to oppose it with unremitting persistence and vigour. These things deserve to be said, and to serve as lessons for the future.

Accordingly, repeating his reply of 3rd March to the urgent requests which the Commander-in-Chief had submitted previously on 28th February, the Minister of the Interior produced a lengthy memorandum dated 20th August defending himself to the Minister of War against the charges he felt were being brought against him for his negligent direction of the Security Department. While it might, he agreed, be true that over the past few weeks the amount of information supplied to the Commander-in-Chief had decreased, this was because "since the outbreaks in June, the state of morale in the country had happily improved and the propaganda efforts of the pacifists had very significantly diminished. . . ." Then, repeating his attempt of 3rd March to break off all direct contact with the Commander-in-Chief, he proposed that all information in future should be supplied by his services to a Liaison Officer attached to the Ministry of War and that the Special Commissioners – except, of course, those in the army zones – should no longer submit reports to the military authorities direct, the Prefects alone being qualified to do this. These measures, he observed, should do whatever was required "to dispel all traces of the misunderstanding which appeared to have arisen between the High Command and the Security Department, for reasons unknown to the latter. . ."

Having read this apologia, which the Minister of War reported to him in a letter of 23rd August, *the Commander-in-Chief returned to the charge in a letter of 27th August – not in any useless attempt to define his responsibilities but to bring home the incompetence of a vitally important service and to see it speedily reformed.* He stated that he had received no reports from the Security Department during the months of May and June when the crisis was at its height. Nor had he had those of the Prefect of Police, the Prefect of the Loire and the Prefect of the Bouches-du-Rhône, which were extremely important and contained specially valuable information about centres of unrest in the interior. All he knew about the pacifist meetings was what he was able to read about them in "L'Humanité" and the "Journal du Peuple". The criminal propaganda of the news-sheet "Vague" was not made known to him, and he was not able to take stock of the harm it was doing, until its extensive circulation among the men had already contaminated the army at many points.

As for the proposal that the Commander-in-Chief should have no further communication with the Security Department except through a Liaison Officer attached to the office of the Minister of War, this would mean a sacrifice on the Commander-in-Chief's side of all the advantages which he could expect from personal contact: the power to ensure that no document would be delayed by those transmitting it: rapidity of information; the benefit of verbal explanations.

Despite his repeated efforts, it was only gradually that the Commander-in-Chief obtained acceptance of his principal demands. He managed to preserve his right to direct weekly access to the Minister of the Interior, but had no success, throughout the whole of the summer, in getting the centres of agitation extirpated root and branch. Thus it was that on 23rd September he was once more addressing the Minister of War on the harm done at the front by the circulation of the "Bonnet Rouge", and the bad effects of this journal on the morale of its regular readers.

Control of the national Press

Being powerless to take the firm action he would have liked against these organs of defeatism, *the Commander-in-Chief turned his attention to the national Press*, fortunately the largest and most influential section of newspapers, *and attempted to steer it along the right path*. His aim was to persuade it to ban all pessimistic articles and, while obviously not overdoing it, to act as the mouthpiece of a spirit of healthy optimism.

To this end, "Press missions" were set up in July. Journalists and writers, with officers acting as guides, were taken on visits to units at interesting points of the front. Their articles, which gained in accuracy as a result, were submitted at GHQ to the scrutiny of officers appointed by the Commander-in-Chief and acting on his directions. The "copy" then passed to the Censor's office in Paris, now reorganised on lines acceptable to the Commander-in-Chief and in accordance with his views.

Since the Press did not always take kindly to this guidance and control, the Commander-in-Chief had to return to the subject on many occasions in his letters to the Minister of War. "It is essential", he wrote on 23rd August, "that what the troops read in the newspapers should provide them with grounds for perseverance and enthusiasm and not for scepticism and bitterness. . . . Tactful direction must be applied to the Press to persuade it to be less critical and more factual in its reports, and to remember that the blank spaces resulting from the Censor's excisions only leave the reader free, in a very harmful way, to imagine goodness knows what. . . ." On 20th October he expressed a wish that the newspapers should devote less space to their favourite theme of "our victorious army" and more to articles which placed due emphasis on "the ever increasing weight of our allies' contribution and the certain prospect of a victorious peace which could alone be counted on to bring general prosperity and ensure the recovery of our industry, trade and agriculture". On 30th November he underlined the danger of giving too much publicity to the Courts Martial then in progress, and to events in Russia, which had a demoralising effect.

The Commander-in-Chief continued to send the Government such suggestions right up to the end of the war, in a constant effort to prevent the nerves of the soldiers, now raw with weariness, from being harmfully worked upon. And when publications detrimental to morale slipped through the Censor's net in Paris and percolated through from the interior to the armies, they were seized in accordance with detailed regulations brought to the notice of Army Group commanders in Notes of 7th and 15th October, 1917.

Reform of tactical training

Gradually cured of an illness which had almost destroyed it, and protected against a recurrence of the disease, the army now needed to be brought up to concert pitch for the next round of the struggle.

Its retraining to a point where it was once more fit for battle was the object of *Directive No. 2 of 20th June.* To indicate the substance of this document in a few words, it declared that, as the latest operations had once again proved, a unit will give what its training has equipped it to give. Nothing is more calculated to inspire the soldier with confidence than his ability to handle his complex equipment with ease and skill, but if the necessary progress was to be made in this direction the assistance of specialist instructors would be required, since no unit commander can be an expert in everything, nor will his duties leave him sufficient time to make a detailed study of all the new weapons. Courses for specialists, on essentially practical lines, would, accordingly, be conducted in "schools" or "classes" attached to training centres equipped with all the necessary resources. The training would be completed by participation in large-scale joint exercises. The units involved in these would wherever possible be sent to camps where they could carry out manoeuvres *based closely on battle conditions* and leaving as little as possible to the imagination. The specialists would operate with their units in the normal way, and detailed study would be given in particular to liaison between the various arms.

Senior officers, regimental and brigade commanders and general officers, would also have the opportunity to brush up their technical knowledge by taking part occasionally in exercises in "centres" set up for the purpose, under the direction of the army group commanders, on 1st July.

In this way, *the training of all officers would be reorganised* from top to bottom of the scale, restoring the army's self-confidence after its recent tribulations and enabling it to profit by the experience gained from its misfortunes.

CONCLUSION

THE CURE AND ITS RESULTS

The Commander-in-Chief followed from day to day the progress of the cure he had prescribed to put the army firmly back on its feet, and behind it the nation.

By the middle of June there was already an improvement, manifested by the decrease in the number of acts of indiscipline, and a sharp reaction among those who had remained sound throughout and who condemned the folly of the mutineers. "After three years of fighting, hardship, and misery," ran one soldier's letter, "it would really be too bad if these outbreaks of impatience were permitted to lead to the escape of our prey, just when he is on the point of falling into our hands!"

In August only four cases of indiscipline took place at the front, though unrest still continued to a certain extent at stations and on leave trains. Most important, however, the Paris region was now calm, and the improvement there seemed complete – a fact to which the Commander-in-Chief drew the War Minister's attention in a letter of 14th August.

By September, confidence in the High Command was apparent everywhere.

The Intelligence Service of GHQ reported in October that the postal censorship produced the following information: "Morale excellent in 24% of all units; good in 71%; mediocre in only 5%. Inadequate quantity of the rations complained about in only 15% of units; quality in 12%. Standard of clothing criticised in only 10% of units; camps and billets in 12%; dugouts in 5%. The new leave system is proving extremely popular." The cheerful behaviour of the men in rest areas exerted a good influence on the

civilian population and was reflected in a corresponding improvement in morale at home.

On 23rd October *a definite turning-point was marked by the brilliant tactical success at Malmaison,* planned and carried through in
accordance with the methods laid down in Directive No. 1.

812 field guns, 862 heavy guns, 105 long-range guns and 66
trench batteries supported six divisions placed in advanced positions along a front of 10 to 12 kilometres. Bombardment on an
almost unlimited scale continued solidly for four days before the
attack, cowing the defenders, isolating them from their rear,
depriving them of sleep and making it impossible for rations, reinforcements or reliefs to be sent up to them. The French Air Force
was out in strength and dominated the battlefield completely.

When the infantry advanced to attack in accordance with a
meticulously planned time-table, it had, in addition to its own
machine-gun effectives, a supporting force of 37-millimetre guns,
Stokes mortars with their trench gun crews, and tanks – all
capable of wiping out any pockets of resistance which had sur-
vived the effects of the preliminary barrages.

In less than forty-eight hours, all the objectives had been
attained. Our losses, it is true, amounted to 14,000 men, including
the lightly wounded. But the German killed and wounded were
estimated at 40,000, to which must be added 11,500 prisoners
brought in by our men, with 200 guns, 222 *minenwerfer*, and 720
machine guns.

During the last few days of October, immediately after this
action, the postal censorship showed that the units who had participated were *quite intoxicated by their victory.* They were thrilled
to have made such an excellent catch, "with light losses considering the extent of the success". As one of them wrote: "The morale
of the troops is wonderful. . . . There is singing on the march and
we are all very cheerful. . . . The Boches are completely demoral-
ized. . . . If the war was as successful along the whole front as it is
here, there'd soon be no Boches left. . . . We are filthy, muddy,
we stink to high heaven, but we are proud. . . . This is a victory
all right!"

In short, *by adapting our methods to the circumstances of the hour, better training, more confident team-work by commanders and their subordinates in accomplishing their common task, such remarkable results were achieved that the crisis was now definitely and permanently at an end.*

There were, however, one or two troubles still ahead. . . .

The end of November saw a sharp new assault on morale. The Pope's peace moves, the Stockholm, London and Berne conferences, and the Bordeaux congress revived pacifist undercurrents, and the army was once more flooded with leaflets. This evil propaganda exploited the approach of winter, the deplorable impression made by the treason trials,[1] the situation in Russia, the disastrous defeat of the Italian army,[2] the delay in the arrival of American reinforcements, and the severe restrictions imposed on the civilian population. The enemy did all in his power to encourage these efforts, for if the first signs of the earlier crisis had escaped his attention, this time he knew everything. He managed to see to it that his pamphlets and newspapers – such as the celebrated "Gazette des Ardennes" – were circulated in the French front line and at the rear. He instigated conversations with the men in the trenches opposite. He erected placards in front of our lines. He sent over rockets and miniature balloons to bring us news of the armistice on the eastern front and the joint manifesto of Lenin and Trotsky on the subject of immediate peace terms.

In fact, however, the very gravity of the threat only threw into

[1] The trials of Malvy, Joseph Caillaux, a former prime minister, Almereyda, editor of the pacifist and subversive newspaper "Le Bonnet Rouge", Bolo Pasha, an agent in German pay, and others. Malvy, publicly attacked by Clemenceau, was put on trial at his own request. He was charged with allowing "Le Bonnet Rouge" to be subsidised out of public funds (it also received money from Germany), found guilty, and sentenced to a term of exile. [Translator's note.]

[2] The Battle of Caporetto, fought on 24th October, 1917, and the retreat of the Italian army towards the Piave, where it re-formed at the beginning of November.

relief the effectiveness of the cure. Acting this time in full accord with each other, *the French Government[1] and High Command took energetic counter-measures, having learned from the lessons of the summer of 1917 how morale should be maintained.*

Indeed, the spirit of the army was barely ruffled by this storm, and righted itself without having suffered any damage.

Our armies were now ready to be launched into the fierce battles of the spring of 1918. They would withstand the ordeals of 21st March and 27th May without a single moment of weakness; and they would then march steadily and victoriously forward, from 15th July to 11th November, 1918, with a resilience and strength of spirit which should serve as an example to all future generations of Frenchmen.

[1] Ribot, the Prime Minister, had resigned on 7th September, 1917, and been replaced by M. Painlevé, who himself resigned on 13th November, 1917, and was replaced by M. Clemenceau.

General de Gaulle in 1940

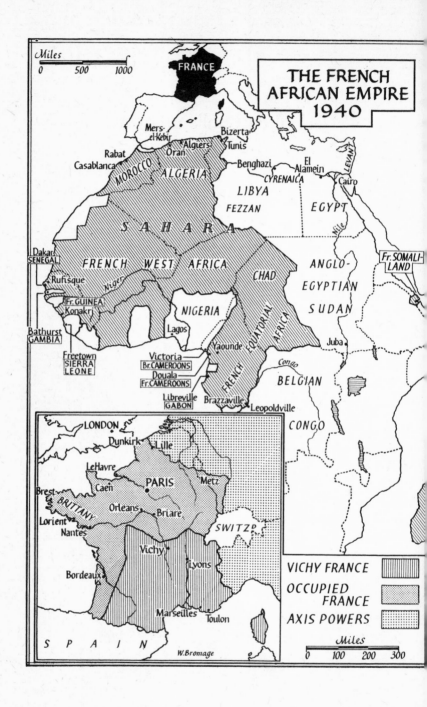

THE FRENCH
AFRICAN EMPIRE
1940

Miles
0   500   1000

FRANCE

Mers-el-Kebir
Rabat
Casablanca
MOROCCO
Oran   Algiers
ALGERIA   Tunis   Bizerta
Benghazi   El Alamein
CYRENAICA
LIBYA   Cairo
FEZZAN   EGYPT

S A H A R A

Dakar
SENEGAL
FRENCH   WEST   AFRICA   CHAD
ANGLO-
EGYPTIAN
SUDAN
Rufisque
Niger
Fr. GUINEA
Konakri
NIGERIA   Juba
Bathurst
GAMBIA   Lagos
Freetown
SIERRA
LEONE   Yaounde
Victoria
Br. CAMEROONS
Douala
Fr. CAMEROONS   FRENCH EQUATORIAL AFRICA
Congo
BELGIAN
Libreville
GABON   Brazzaville   Leopoldville
CONGO

Fr. SOMALI-LAND
LEVANT

LONDON
Dunkirk   Lille
LeHavre
Caen   PARIS   Metz
Brest   BRITTANY
Orleans   Briare
Lorient   SWITZ?
Nantes
Vichy
Lyons
Bordeaux
Marseilles   Toulon
S P A I N
W. Bromage

VICHY FRANCE
OCCUPIED
FRANCE
AXIS POWERS

Miles
0   100   200   300

I

On the 17th June, 1940, the day the government of Monsieur Paul Reynaud resigned and Marshal Pétain headed a ministry to ask the Germans for an armistice, I brought General de Gaulle from Bordeaux to England in my plane.

A few days later, de Gaulle was recognised by His Majesty's Government, and I was appointed Head of the Spears Mission responsible for all matters concerning his relationship and that of the Free French with the British government and authorities.

For the de Gaulle I then knew, and whose problems as far as they concerned Britain it was my duty to assess and understand, I have an admiration and respect subsequent events have in no way affected.

Without him there would have been no Free French movement, and, although later I differed with him so deeply, I am convinced that France owes her salvation to him as, in the First World War, she owed it to Pétain.

The very faults and defects which were so trying to those who attempted to help de Gaulle were to reveal themselves as the very structure of his success.

The little I had seen of de Gaulle before the 17th June, and all I had heard of him, mainly from Monsieur Paul Reynaud, had greatly impressed me, and I had been disconcerted and disappointed when, on arriving in London, I was taken to task by everyone, including the Prime Minister, for not having brought over a well-known French political personage, someone who could influence world opinion and rally such elements of resistance as existed in France. My answer was simple: there was literally no one else at Bordeaux, where all the French political forces were gathered, who would come. De Gaulle was the only one. People at home, even the best informed, had no idea of what a cesspool of defeatism Bordeaux had become; and French politics being what they were, had a leader of the Right appeared in England, the entire Left of the French population would have opposed him, using his political complexion as a pretext for not resisting the Germans. Exactly the same thing would have happened, but the other way round, had a politician of the Left attempted to rally his countrymen. I argued that it was far better to start writing this chapter of history on a blank page, and I guaranteed that, given a reasonable sum of money, de Gaulle's name would be known to every newspaper the world over in six months' time. This was in fact achieved in collaboration with Desmond Morton, the Prime Minister's personal assistant, at a cost of well under £1,000, thanks to the disinterested services of Mr Richmond Temple, the publicity consultant. The operation, however, revealed one side of de Gaulle's character which drove poor Temple wild. He would not have his photograph taken, or help a talented man write a book about him, or give interviews. Seldom in history had a politico-military leader been so allergic to publicity.

When I took de Gaulle to see Churchill at No. 10 Downing Street, the day we arrived in London from Bordeaux, one of the first things he asked the Prime Minister was for permission to broadcast to France over the BBC. Churchill gave his consent without a moment's hesitation. His first impulse was certainly the generous one of responding to the request of the fugitive and lone French adherent to our cause, but he certainly also thought that whether de Gaulle turned out to be a good or a bad broadcaster the mere fact that even one French voice proclaimed resistance would be useful and might awaken echoes in unexpected quarters.

Although this first broadcast is so well known, I give the text for the benefit of English readers.

"Les chefs qui, depuis de nombreuses années, sont à la tête des armées françaises, ont formé un gouvernement.

"Ce gouvernement, alléguant la défaite de nos armées, s'est mis en rapport avec l'ennemi pour cesser le combat.

"*Certes, nous avons été, nous sommes, submergés par la force mécanique, terrestre et aérienne, de l'ennemi.*

"*Infiniment plus que leur nombre, ce sont les chars, les avions, la tactique des Allemands qui nous font reculer. Ce sont les chars, les avions, la tactique des Allemands qui ont surpris nos chefs au point de les amener là où ils en sont aujourd'hui.*

"*Mais le dernier mot est-il dit? L'espérance doit-elle disparaître? La défaite est-elle définitive? Non!*

"*Croyez-moi, moi qui vous parle en connaissance de cause et vous dis que rien n'est perdu pour la France. Les mêmes moyens qui nous ont vaincus peuvent faire venir un jour la victoire.*

"*Car la France n'est pas seule! Elle n'est pas seule! Elle n'est pas seule! Elle a un vaste Empire derrière elle. Elle peut faire bloc avec l'Empire britannique qui tient la mer et continue la lutte. Elle peut, comme l'Angleterre, utiliser sans limites l'immense industrie des États-Unis.*

"*Cette guerre n'est pas limitée au territoire malheureux de notre pays. Cette guerre n'est pas tranchée par la bataille de France. Cette guerre est une guerre mondiale. Toutes les fautes, tous les retards, toutes les souffrances, n'empêchent pas qu'il y a, dans l'univers, tous les moyens nécessaires pour écraser un jour nos ennemis. Foudroyés aujourd'hui par la force mécanique, nous pourrons vaincre dans l'avenir par une force mécanique supérieure. Le destin du monde est là.*

"*Moi, Général de Gaulle, actuellement à Londres, j'invite les officiers et les soldats français qui se trouvent en territoire britannique ou qui viendraient à s'y trouver, avec leurs armes ou sans leurs armes, j'invite les ingénieurs et les ouvriers spécialistes des industries d'armement qui se trouvent en territoire britannique ou qui viendraient à s'y trouver, à se mettre en rapport avec moi.*

"*Quoi qu'il arrive, la flamme de la résistance française ne doit pas s'éteindre et ne s'éteindra pas.*

"*Demain, comme aujourd'hui, je parlerai à la Radio de Londres.*"[1]

[1] "The leaders who, for many years past, have been at the head of the French armed forces, have set up a government.

"Alleging the defeat of our armies, this government has entered into negotiations with the enemy with a view to bringing about a cessation of hostilities. It is quite true that we were, and still are, overwhelmed by enemy mechanised

Next day, the 19th, de Gaulle came into my office at St Stephen's House, and after congratulating him on his broadcast I said, "Will you be speaking again tonight, *mon Général*?" "*Je parle tous les jours*" – "I speak every day," he answered, and he did speak again on the 19th. But Jean Monnet, who had been the chief French representative on the Anglo-French Co-ordinating Committee and, when this was dissolved, on the formation of the Pétain Government, was given a post at the Foreign Office, persuaded Lord Halifax that de Gaulle should not be allowed to broadcast daily. So on the 20th and 21st June he was prevented from speaking. Protests by Duff Cooper and myself were overridden by the Foreign Office. We felt so strongly that it was

---

forces, both on the ground and in the air. It was the tanks, the planes, and the tactics of the Germans, far more than the fact that we were outnumbered, that forced our armies to retreat. It was the German tanks, planes, and tactics that provided the element of surprise which brought our leaders to their present plight.

"But has the last word been said? Must we abandon all hope? Is our defeat final and irremediable? To those questions I answer – No!

"Speaking in full knowledge of the facts, I ask you to believe me when I say that the cause of France is not lost. The very factors that brought about our defeat may one day lead us to victory.

"For, remember this, France does not stand alone. She is not isolated. Behind her is a vast empire, and she can make common cause with the British Empire, which commands the seas and is continuing the struggle. Like England, she can draw unreservedly on the immense industrial resources of the United States.

"This war is not limited to our unfortunate country. The outcome of the struggle has not been decided by the battle of France. This is a world war. Mistakes have been made, there have been delays and untold suffering, but the fact remains that there still exists in the world everything we need to crush our enemies some day. Today we are crushed by the sheer weight of mechanised force hurled against us, but we can still look to a future in which even greater mechanised force will bring us victory. The destiny of the world is at stake.

"I, General de Gaulle, now in London, call on all French officers and men who are at present on British soil, or may be in the future, with or without their arms; I call on all engineers and skilled workmen from the armaments factories who are at present on British soil, or may be in the future, to get in touch with me.

"Whatever happens, the flame of French resistance must not and shall not die.

"Tomorrow I shall broadcast again from London."

disastrous to silence the only voice that spoke for French resistance that on the afternoon of the 22nd we telephoned independently of each other to Churchill, who was at Chequers. He was deeply concerned and not a little amazed by what I told him, not least perhaps by the fact that this action negatived his own permission. He told me he would call a meeting of the cabinet for nine o'clock that evening, de Gaulle was to bring the text of what he wanted to say, and, if the cabinet approved, he could deliver it on the BBC that night.

So de Gaulle came to 10 Downing Street in a taxi with my secretary, with his text in French. She dictated a translation into English to one of the Downing Street typists as the cabinet assembled. The urgency was such that one of the prime minister's secretaries took each page as it was typed into the cabinet room. There was indeed no time to spare if de Gaulle was to broadcast that night. A carbon copy of the speech was brought to de Gaulle and me in the room adjoining the cabinet where we were waiting. We made only verbal corrections. The text was approved by the cabinet without demur within ten minutes, and de Gaulle drove from Downing Street to the BBC and was on the air at 10 pm.

Thereafter he broadcast, not every day but generally at intervals of two days during the rest of June, and less frequently but regularly in July, and there was no further attempt by Monnet to stop him.

But the first head-on clashes I remember did occur quite soon over these same broadcasts when the Foreign Office asked to see de Gaulle's text before he delivered it.

"Has the Foreign Office cleared the text?" asked the BBC. "Otherwise we cannot transmit. To do so would contravene our orders."

Now it was natural enough that the Foreign Office should insist on nothing being said over our official transmission that might contravene government policy, but over his broadcasts de Gaulle quite rightly would not accept any form of control. He flatly refused to submit his text to either censorship or inspection. How could he claim to be free if he did? How could he otherwise have repudiated the accusation by Vichy that he was a British stooge? Either he could speak freely to the French people or he would not speak at all. On this he would never give way. Both sides were right and justified in their attitude, but it was very difficult. My sympathies were with de Gaulle, but a new approach had to be thought out on each occasion. I would inform the general of the matters our government trusted he would not mention and he doubtless realised that if he did not accept these hints the talk might be cut or further transmission refused. There were occasions when, within ten minutes of his being due to broadcast, I was still seeking a compromise.

2

Before the end of June the government, and in particular the prime minister, were fast becoming convinced that it was the fact, however unpalatable, that no important French politician, no leader, would defy the Nazis with anything less than three thousand miles of ocean between himself and them. The Channel proved too narrow for many of those Frenchmen who had crossed it, and they joined the queue of those more anxious to salute the Statue of Liberty in person and in situ than to indulge in the dangerous occupation of striking a blow for what that statue stood for. Few of these travellers may have recollected that it was France, the fountainhead of freedom, that had presented this monument to the USA.

The fact that no Frenchman of standing would come to England soon became glaringly obvious even to those who persistently substituted their illusory and distorted picture of France for the reality. When Duff Cooper and Lord Gort were sent on the dangerous mission of trying to contact Georges Mandel and others who had been allowed to sail for North Africa in the *Massilia*, they found their quarry had been put under arrest and were incommunicado. They themselves were compelled by the

Vichy officials in Rabat to leave Morocco forthwith without discharging their mission.

On the 23rd June the British government gave full vent to its indignation and sorrow and defined its attitude in the following statement:

His Majesty's Government have heard with grief and amazement that the terms dictated by the Germans have been accepted by the French Government at Bordeaux. They cannot feel that such, or similar terms, could have been submitted to by any French Government which possessed freedom, independence and constitutional authority. Such terms, if accepted by all Frenchmen, would place, not only France, but the French Empire, entirely at the mercy and in the power of the German and Italian Dictators. Not only would the French people be held down and forced to work against their Ally, not only would the soil of France be used with the approval of the Bordeaux Government as the means of attacking their Ally, but the whole resources of the French Empire and of the French Navy would speedily pass into the hands of the adversary for the fulfilment of his purpose.

His Majesty's Government firmly believe that, whatever happens, they will be able to carry the war wherever it may lead, on the seas, in the air and upon land, to a successful conclusion. When Great Britain is victorious, she will, in spite of the action of the Bordeaux Government, cherish the cause of the French people, and a British victory is the only possible hope for the restoration of the greatness of France and the freedom of its people. Brave men from other countries overrun by the Nazi invasion are steadfastly fighting in the ranks of freedom.

Accordingly, His Majesty's Government call upon all Frenchmen outside the power of the enemy to aid them in their task, and thereby render its accomplishment more sure and swift. They appeal to all Frenchmen wherever they may be, to aid to the utmost of their strength the forces of liberation, which are enormous, and which, faithfully and resolutely used, will assuredly prevail.

General de Gaulle thereupon published an agreed statement announcing the formation of a French National Committee for the following purposes:

The French National Committee will account for its acts either to the legal and established French Government, as soon as such a one exists, or to the representatives of the people as soon as circumstances allow them to assemble in conditions compatible with liberty, dignity and security. It will take under its jurisdiction all French citizens at present on British territory, and will assume the direction of all military and administrative bodies who are now, or may in the future, be in this country. The French National Committee will get in touch with such bodies in order to call for their participation in its formation. The war is not lost, the country is not dead, hope is not extinct. *Vive la France!*

His Majesty's Government then published a further statement as follows:

His Majesty's Government find that the terms of the armistice just signed, in contravention of agreements solemnly made between the Allied Governments, reduce the Bordeaux Government to a state of complete subjection to the enemy and deprive it of all liberty and all right to represent free French citizens. His Majesty's Government therefore now declare that they can no longer regard the Bordeaux Government as the Government of an independent country. His Majesty's Government have taken note of the proposal to form a Provisional French National Committee fully representing independent French elements determined on the prosecution of the war in fulfilment of the international obligations of France. His Majesty's Government declare that they will recognise such a Provisional French National Committee, and will deal with them in all matters concerning the prosecution of the war, so long as that

Committee continues to represent all French elements resolved to fight the common enemy.

They had not yet heard of the failure of the Duff Cooper Mission and still hoped that some representative Frenchmen would rally to de Gaulle. Previously, on the 19th June, de Gaulle had telegraphed to General Noguès, C.-in-C. of North Africa and Resident General in Morocco, offering to place himself under his orders if he rejected the armistice, and on the 24th he telegraphed to him again in the same sense. He also sent messages to all the proconsuls of France's vast empire suggesting the formation of a Defence Committee. He did not suggest that he should be its leader; in the France of that time for so junior a man to have done so would have merely covered him with ridicule. He merely offered himself, being in London, as a convenient liaison link with the British. For a very short time it seemed as if some at least of these highly placed Frenchmen would revolt against the armistice terms, and had General Noguès done so many would have followed him, but none did except Le Gentilhomme in French Somaliland, whose faithful loyalty to his British ally never wavered, and Catroux, who had been dismissed by the Vichy Government as governor-general in Indo-China. All the rest accepted the dismal lead of Pétain and fell in behind him to swell the funeral procession of their own country, of which *Monsieur le Maréchal* was the decrepit pall-bearer, together with a few more such as Laval, Darlan, etc.

This lack of support of Frenchmen, together with the complete failure of the Duff Cooper Mission and the expulsion of our chief liaison officer from Algiers, at last convinced the British government that de Gaulle provided the only active support they could bank on, so the idea of a French National Committee was abandoned, and on the 28th June the following communiqué was published:

His Majesty's Government recognises General de Gaulle as Leader of all Free Frenchmen, wherever they may be, who rally to him in support of the Allied Cause.

The Prime Minister appointed me to be head of the mission to de Gaulle as soon as he was recognised officially. Contacts with many departments had to be established. It may only have been a friendly gesture on de Gaulle's part, or it may be that from this moment he was beginning to outline in his mind the course he would follow when he asked that I be appointed 'Ambassador' to him. The only people who had so far taken him seriously were Marshal Pétain, now head of the French state, and General Weygand, the head of the French army, who condemned him to death, thus early revealing their fear of the forces he might unleash in opposition to the white flag of surrender they had hoisted.

For the first few days the mission was known as the 'British Mission to General de Gaulle', but at a small meeting in General Ismay's office, then at Richmond Terrace, in early July, it was christened the 'Spears Mission' and from that time on was never known as anything else. It was made responsible for relations with de Gaulle and any organisation he might be able to create. I was given the inestimable privilege of communicating direct with the cabinet secretariat and the Prime Minister.

The role the Spears Mission was called upon to play was not an easy one. There was not a trace of a base on which to build, and de Gaulle had no resources other than the 100,000 francs in cash given him by Paul Reynaud at Bordeaux.

Where was de Gaulle to work? Not in the defence departments. Security forbade that, besides which at the Admiralty a French naval mission still adhering to Vichy was installed. So I put him into a suite of bare rooms in St Stephen's House where I had long had a private office. Then a hunt started to find a modicum of simple furniture.

What de Gaulle felt I never knew, but I found it heart-breaking to note that his call to his compatriots inspired practically no response among the large French population of London. Men of substance did not flock to him. There were no queues of callers. Some simple men, mostly sailors I think, did arrive and for their benefit a cask of red wine was broached at the Embankment entrance of St Stephen's House.

Looking at de Gaulle's few collaborators, I had to get what comfort there was to be gathered from the quip Clemenceau once made about his government: "you must remember it was not eagles that saved the Capitol."

The English on the whole were sympathetic, admiring and quite grateful to this solitary champion of their cause, although his unique adhesion served to expose the absence of armed legions rushing to their support. His critics were among the French, and the more individuals felt the lash his courage inflicted on their cowardice the more bitter they were, and the French are really experts at denigration. Some dubbed him an adventurer, others a charlatan, every tale that had attached to him as a not very popular officer was dug up and rehearsed and some averred that his motive power was resentment against "Marshal Pétain for having put him in his place".

As the interests of France were practically universal and the only standard bearer of these was now de Gaulle, a number of departments were represented at the Spears Mission, which was allocated the greater part of Gwydyr House in Whitehall, and there I realised for the first time that, although as a Member of Parliament for many years I had considered myself an inhabitant of that district, I had co-existed with a world which had been as invisible to me as might have been a population of ghosts. Officials were, I knew, the denizens of the great departments of state. In the House, when it was in session, you sometimes caught sight of them in their boxes ready to supply their ministers with information at short notice, and we all realised some of them were busy concocting their chiefs' answers to parliamentary questions. But now, for the first time as far as I was concerned, they suddenly emerged from their hitherto imperceptible world as potent beings who sallied forth for a moment from obscure hideouts down long bleak corridors along which they would presently disappear again. They were revealed as possessing great powers, exercised, I soon began to think, in the main in thwarting each other. They seemed to hunt in packs in the sense that one always seemed to need the agreement of someone else to do anything, but hardly had a couple or two got off on the scent when a rival posse would appear from an unsuspected quarter and cross the trail.

I then understood as I never had in the House why so many ministers infinitely preferred an occasional rough house in the Commons when presenting their estimates or answering questions to falling out with their departments. What did it matter being badgered for an hour or two by tiresome members if the reward was a whole year of pampered protection at the hands of a sympathetic ministry which well understood the value of a minister who responded to the gentle and tactful prodding of his civil servants? Their motto might have been that of the Prussian Junkers of old who declared: "Our king we shall obey – if he will do what we say."

All this was gradually revealed when I found myself in a fine office, with smart messengers who politely informed me I could get neither ink nor paper without somebody's authority. Even red tape was unobtainable without written sanction.

Mr Henry Hopkinson[1] of the Foreign Office undertook to find de Gaulle accommodation, and quite soon this efficient and resourceful man had installed him at what was to be his permanent headquarters in Carlton House Gardens.

All the members of my mission were devoted to the cause they were now working for, to help those Frenchmen who would fight on, to keep what was left of the French empire in the war, in other words to help de Gaulle in every way they could. And there was also a spur to avert a danger which I was more alive to than others, the possibility of what the French themselves called the 'renversement des alliances', which, more crudely put, meant repudiating the British alliance and concluding one with the Nazis against us.

Such a policy would have revolted many, perhaps the great majority of Frenchmen, but fine words would have been woven into a thick cloth of deception to make the French public believe that it was rendered inevitable by the horrible way Great Britain

[1] Now Lord Colyton.

had abandoned France, even withholding at the last what was
left of her air force which might, who knows, have saved the
French army.

How narrowly we escaped the terrible danger of the 'renversement des alliances' is shown by the following incident.

In my book on the fall of France[1] I describe a dinner I attended
at Briare on the 12th June, 1940, as the guest of the French military mission to our GHQ. My hosts were well bred and, I believed,
convinced Anglophiles. Some time after my book had been published I was the guest in France of one of these officers. Although his
family had been gallicised for generations, some of his forebears
having held high office in Paris, he looked a typical Englishman
even in French uniform, and, unlike a few other Frenchmen I
have met of either English or Irish descent, was proud of his
English breeding and liked nothing better than hunting in the
shires. One day he asked me if I knew what had happened at the
mess at Briare when I had left it for the presidential train. "No,
do tell me." "As soon as you had gone, to my intense disquiet,"
he said, "a discussion was started as to whether France should remain in the war or not. Powerful arguments were put forward in
support of and against either solution. The views were so evenly
divided that it was decided to take a vote of the officers present."
It was "a close-run thing", there was only a majority of two for
continuing in the war. Having been miserably anxious during the
whole proceedings, my friend was greatly relieved at the result.
He jumped up and said, "So now we have taken our decision,
let's start off and join the British forces tomorrow." But he was
severely reproved by practically all. "You do not seem to have
understood the purpose and meaning of our vote," they said.
"What we have decided is that we shall remain in the British
alliance and will not repudiate it. Had the vote gone the other
way we would have considered ourselves to be free to conclude an
alliance with Germany."

Although unaware at the time of this startling piece of information, I knew well how delicately poised was French opinion and

[1] *Assignment to Catastrophe* 1954, Heinemann.

how easy it would have been to mislead the utterly forlorn and miserable French nation, then feeling, no doubt, as did the in-inhabitants of a Greek town of antiquity suddenly finding themselves, after defeat, herded together and handed over to the tender mercies of the slave merchants. And it was because of these fears that from the day of my return to London I pleaded the cause of creating a French force on British territory.

Seeing de Gaulle daily and working with him closely I came to know him well. The first and obvious thing about him was that he was a gentleman and an honourable man, though it presently emerged that when dealing with what he held to be the interests of France he felt released from the ordinary rules of rectitude or fair play, nor were any holds then barred. He was incapable of doing anything personally dishonourable and would always have preferred the truth to a lie, but when defending the cause of France as he saw it he gave the impression of having studied diplomacy at the court of Cesare Borgia. This impression was enhanced by hooded eyes, an elephantine nose and a long ivory-coloured face which might well have rested on a ruff.

He had a powerful imagination, but it was a military and political one, and I do not think he deigned to nurse visions of himself as a great historic figure. His one ambition was to serve the goddess he revered more than all the saints in heaven – France.

The fear of making any agreement that might weaken France in the future stood over him in merciless tyranny. To this secretly very religious man to compromise on this must have stood for eternal damnation.

A fundamental, a very French distrust of Britain and of the British had serious and lasting effects on his attitude to us and to the prime minister. He could neither understand nor accept that when we said we had no territorial ambitions at France's expense, we meant it, nor believe that we would not somehow, sometime, succumb to the temptation to help ourselves to a tempting morsel of the French empire.

And supposing perfidious Albion really imposed on herself the self-denying ordinance of not cutting off a steak from the body of her weakened partner, was it not at least possible that the war might end in a compromise, and sections of the French empire be thrown into the scales to redeem British possessions? This mistrust appeared very early, and explains why de Gaulle insisted, during the negotiations for an agreement with the British, even before he had established any semblance of power and authority, that the British government should guarantee the integral re-establishment of the frontiers of both metropolitan France and her empire. The fact that the British authorities demurred at binding themselves, at the very moment they were under the threat of invasion and when survival was more a matter of hope than of conviction, intensified de Gaulle's intransigence, the reason for which only dawned on us later.

The argument over the text of the agreement between His Majesty's Government and de Gaulle was conducted with exasperating acerbity on the latter's behalf by his tiresome bearded legal adviser, Professor Cassin, until even the best disposed of Foreign Office officials grew weary of trying to meet what appeared to be this manifestation of the overwrought nerves of our guests. Finally the Prime Minister informed de Gaulle that Britain would promise the integral restoration of the independence and grandeur of France and that was all we could possibly under-take at this stage, but when the agreement was concluded and signed by Churchill and de Gaulle at Chequers on the 7th August it was accompanied by a 'secret' letter from the prime minister which explained that Great Britain could not "guarantee" the restoration of the territorial frontiers of metropolitan France and its dependencies "but, naturally, we will do our best".

In his reply, de Gaulle expressed the hope that "one day the British government would consider this question with less reserve".

Nevertheless I do not think it occurred to Churchill or to any other member of the government or any high official that our guest did not believe what we said and that there lingered a belief in some French quarters that what we were doing for the Free French movement was similar to the effort and expense incurred by a chef, intent on fattening a promising goose.

In those early days de Gaulle was essentially likeable, but soon developed a dislike of being liked as if it were a weakness, as if an acknowledgement of friendliness was to concede to someone a hold over him, so much so that there were times when he tried hard to foster dislike by indulging in deliberate rudeness.

He certainly suffered personal torture when he found that his wife and children had not arrived in England as he had directed. When he told me of this I naturally felt deep sympathy. My wife was also lost in central France with her ambulance, but I said nothing. Indeed I felt another and deeper concern, about which I spoke to the prime minister. If Madame de Gaulle and her children were in German hands, what pressure could not be put on the general, and what use would a man subjected to such stresses be to us? Had I known him better I would have realised it would have made no difference at all. But it was not a risk to run.

The Prime Minister realised the position to the full and authorised the use of one of our very few flying boats, a Sunderland (there were then only three available, I think), to find and bring over Madame de Gaulle. It failed to do so and the machine and its crew were lost. General de Gaulle made no comment when he heard. Meanwhile Madame de Gaulle had made her way to Brittany and found room on one of the very last boats to leave for England. On arrival she telephoned her husband. "So you have arrived?" he said. "Take the train to London."

General de Gaulle is very fortunate in his wife. She is a lady of great courage, self-abnegation and quiet charm, who, whatever the circumstances and difficulties, has bent her life and that of her children to fit into the framework set by her husband. His ideals were hers and she saw to it that they were those of her children. She is in every sense a lady who embodies the virtues of the French high bourgeoisie which has always been the solid backbone of France.

De Gaulle proved his greatness by accepting complete solitude, by refusing from the first to share his responsibility with anyone. He never asked for and seldom accepted advice. He grew to like suffering and told me once, as we flew over the Sahara, that he envied and admired the Tuaregs who were for ever thirsty and enjoyed enduring their torment.

His powers of concentration were immense. He would compose the whole of one of his memorable speeches to the French people for the London BBC in his mind and then write it in beautiful French at great speed in an untidy sloppy hand.

Like all people deficient in a sense of humour, to be accused of a lack of it would probably offend him more than any other accusation that could be levelled against him. Brutality, yes, severity, yes, lack of indulgence, yes – but lack of humour! – and he would no doubt see himself laughing almost out loud at that joke he had heard last week! And the fact was that he did laugh wholeheartedly at many a simple joke, for instance, at meals on the way to Dakar, simple schoolboy jokes that evoked a comic picture, when he would repeatedly smack the palm of one hand with the fist of the other. But a joke based on some subtle play of words or of inflection might well awaken his suspicion lest it concealed a meaning which escaped him.

Sensitive in some ways, he was insensitive in others and had a protective shell which saved him from being affected and therefore diverted by other people's judgements. He thus sometimes failed to appreciate that things he said or did might strike others as droll.

The following incident which occurred later the same year illustrates this. He was staying at the Connaught Hotel and had asked me to an excellent dinner, attended by a few guests, in his private sitting-room. As we sat round the gas fire after dinner de Gaulle said suddenly, following a thought unperceived by the others, "I really am Joan of Arc".

The picture this evoked in my mind was funny, and the expression of one or two of the other guests showed that their reaction was the same as mine. I felt that if he made this statement in a wider circle he would be completely misunderstood. Some would laugh, others would be shocked, feeling that such a statement verged on profanity or even sacrilege. It was only later that I realised that the general was justified in drawing a parallel between Saint Joan and himself, since he, with no more support than the Maid had enjoyed, had also set out, almost single-handed, to save France.

But, in the taut atmosphere of the period, it was too much to hope that harassed and anxious officials would grasp the resemblance between the sweet and gentle Maid and the irascible moustached male giant in uniform they had to deal with. So I said, "If I were you, *mon Général*, I would not recall Joan of Arc too often in England. The English adore her, but nevertheless when she is evoked here a slight smell of burning is often perceptible." Nevertheless he repeated the statement on other occasions when I know his meaning was missed. Either a comic impression remained or people thought that here indeed was proof of megalomania.

He often provided me with cause to smile, although perhaps rather sourly, at the method he evolved of treating high-ranking Englishmen. He had not been slow to notice that the British upper classes absolutely detest 'a row' and will do everything to avoid one, in which they differ from their own lower orders with whom a row is inevitable if you attempt to bully or override them or apply to them words which are considered to be unacceptable insults.

Acting on a precedent perfected by practice, General de Gaulle, when he had a really difficult controversial problem to settle with, say, a minister, would sail in looking like thunder. The less sure he was of his ground the more stormy he appeared. He would slam down his *képi* as aggressively as a bull preparing to charge strikes the ground with his hooves, sit down looking furious and sway his head like a cobra. He would then unleash a stream of accusations that were extremely rude to the person or the department concerned and make remarks that were quite intolerable. The Englishman facing him would be intensely embarrassed, then grow angry, but the angrier he grew the more tongue-tied did he become. Whereupon, suddenly, de Gaulle would spring up, seize his cap and say, "I will come to hear your answer at ten tomorrow morning", and stalk out.

At such times I have on occasion spent the evening with the

British target of de Gaulle's wrath. Generally he did not enjoy his dinner, and was obviously thinking of all the things he would have liked to have said but had not, and I guessed that he probably woke in the night rehearsing the phrases with which he would blast the irascible Frenchman next morning.

The next day came and so did ten o'clock, bringing de Gaulle to the same office where, to the bewilderment of the Englishman, he would be all smiles and politeness, positively exuding *bonhomie*. The Englishman was so relieved at not having to produce his carefully rehearsed remarks that there flowed from his lips a cataract of amiability, and he would immediately concede fifty per cent of the general's demands of the previous evening, which was more than the general had reckoned on obtaining.

There were only two ministers impervious to this system, the Prime Minister and Sir John Anderson, later Lord Waverley.

It might be argued that, at this period, no one on the British side had more to endure from de Gaulle than I had. But I never felt aggrieved. Perhaps because, more than most, I realised something of the Calvary he was ascending, condemned to death by his own old chief, Marshal Pétain, the object of obloquy and intrigue from those of his compatriots who, refusing to fight themselves, vented their hatred on the man who did.

But, although he was sometimes very difficult, he never once failed in courtesy to me, and I am sure it was not only because he realised I was unlikely to react kindly to anything else.

Then also, in those days I was almost invariably in complete agreement with him. I think I understood many if not all his subtleties. I appreciated the skill, adroitness and resilience with which he worked towards his objective.

Indeed, then as now, recreating the situation as it then was, I still think that the treatment he received at our hands in those early days engendered and justified the mistrust with which he regarded us and embittered the whole of our relations with him.

That de Gaulle was a difficult man to deal with is a fact, that he became so, or became increasingly so, speedily developing the harshness and irascibility of a character which can never have been without some acerbity, was largely, perhaps entirely, our fault.

Here was a man who had staked everything, much more than his life, his honour, everything he believed in, on the desperate, the forlorn hope of saving France at the moment when it seemed that her long and on the whole brilliant and glorious history was coming to an end in the miasma of shame her republican institutions had brought her to. Here he was, quite alone on foreign soil, abused by his countrymen, condemned to death as a deserter by his chiefs, denounced by his Embassy and by all the powerful and numerous French missions in Britain, utterly dependent for everything on his hosts: what an opportunity this should have given us for sympathy and understanding!

The British people as a whole did sympathise with and give their trust to this solitary figure. But although there were many sympathisers in all strata of the country only one man really understood: Winston Churchill. Without him there would have been no de Gaulle and no Free French. France owes him her existence even more than we do ours.

However critical de Gaulle was of the British authorities, he had the most unstinting admiration for the quiet unobtrusive determination of the British people, every single individual one of them of either sex, who threw their entire being into a struggle which involved the existence of their country. He realised that you might just as well ask an oyster to give up its shell as ask an Englishman to surrender.

I remember how once or twice when he came to our cottage in Berkshire he paid tribute with immense sincerity to the pathetic and touching schemes of defence local patriotism had inspired.

He had noticed the tree by the side of the road on a swivel so that it could be used to bar the way by being lifted on to a post on the other side, makinga barrier four feet high against the invading Hun.

He had also noted how signposts had been removed so as to mislead the invading Germans if they got that far. The stoical acceptance by the native travellers, who got lost without complaint in loyal acceptance of their fellow subjects' patriotic effort, he deemed to be worthy of every respect, the silent proof of faithful resolution, unaware of its futility, but determined to do something. And he also noted how on the railways the names of the stations had been removed in the belief that enemy airmen would be confused by not being able to read them as they flew over. Such touching ignorance of what can be observed from military aircraft he would comment upon on arrival at our cottage, while speculating how passengers ever reached their destination, as fellow travellers might well wish to ascertain they were not being questioned by an enemy agent before giving any information as to what station the train had reached, which might well lead to the required stop being missed.

This was another and a very pleasant and courteous de Gaulle, who could hardly fit into the small and ancient house, and created the same sense of alarm as when Alice grew inordinately tall in Wonderland. You felt inclined to cry with the Queen, "Persons more than a mile high must leave the Court", as the general made to leave one room for another and had to pass under door lintels that had inflicted many a painful blow on my mere six feet.

In those days de Gaulle had very few cards and no trumps. He realised his only chance was to play an aggressive game, overcall his hand, bang the table, and he did so. In the main he gained the impression that we only helped him in so far as it was in our interest to do so, and this was true. But he also suspected that we might throw him over to propitiate Vichy as the USA was doing; and in this he was wrong. When he held no cards he pretended he did, and blackmailed us in the cause of France with a Hitlerian thoroughness.

As it dawned on de Gaulle that we were easily bullied, he bullied us.

Seen in perspective, these clashes were perhaps inevitable. How painful they were none realised better than I did, as I generally found myself in a central position between the hammer and the anvil.

He experienced very bad examples of British vacillation, especially in the matter of recruiting, which to him seemed nothing but examples of that double dealing and duplicity which his education as a Frenchman had prepared him for but in which he had not hitherto really believed. I entirely sympathised with him in this and fought this battle for and with him with all the vigour I possessed.

The position was this: the general had been granted permission by the Prime Minister to recruit from among the French on British soil, including sailors and soldiers, all those who were willing to join him. If they did so they would be treated in every way, pay, pensions and conditions of service, as our own nationals.

There were many French troops in England; all the contingents from Norway; a fine brigade of Chasseurs Alpins, two battalions of the Foreign Legion, and many sailors.

On the day after he was recognised as the head of the Free French, that is on the 19th June, he visited French troops at Trentham Park, notably the Light Mountain Division and two battalions of the Foreign Legion. He arrived back at my house at midnight, tired and very hungry, having had no food all day, but delighted, *"C'est de la bonne troupe,"* he said. ("They are fine troops"), and so they were.

A cold chicken was produced for him from the larder. There was a message from Lord Lloyd asking him to call him up as soon as he arrived, so he went into the library to do so. When he returned he told us that the Colonial Secretary, evidently alerted by the British authorities in West Africa, who were terrified (especially the military) lest anything should be done to upset their Vichy neighbours, at the news that an attempt might be made to rally the French Cameroons to de Gaulle, wanted to know what the juridical position of the Cameroons under French mandate would be in such an eventuality.

"J'ai dit à Lloyd," declared the newly recognised head of the Free French, *"que c'est moi qui prend le mandat du Cameroon."* ("It is I who assume the mandate of the Cameroons." It seemed as easy as devouring that chicken).

A few days later de Gaulle brought the commander of the Light Division, General Béthouart, to see me at St Stephen's House.

I have seldom met a more charming man, young, vigorous and very good looking. I have, however, felt for years on this occasion I missed a cue and a great opportunity. It seemed to me later that de Gaulle had perhaps meant me to invite my visitor to remain on in England fighting at our side. I did not do so, feeling this was such a personal question, one of individual honour, that no stranger had the right to intervene save when it was a question of explaining the conditions of service we had to offer, and General Béthouart knew these and that he would be welcome. Later, at the time of the American landings in Morocco, he showed his support for the Allies at great risk to himself. Still, it would have been better had he rallied in 1940, and it is possible that a little persuasion would have helped him to decide to do so.

Only once did I break the rule I had imposed on myself of not attempting to stand between a man and his conscience. This was in the case of the diplomat son of a French officer I had loved and admired in the first war. But when he explained his responsibility to a large family of women and children in France, I realised that these were not really questions on which a foreigner, however well intentioned, had the right to express a view.

During this trip to Trentham Park de Gaulle met Lieut.-Colonel Maigrin Verneret, alias Monclar, and his adjutant, Captain Koenig, of the Foreign Legion. The colonel, fair, fresh-skinned very closely shaved, bespectacled and soft-voiced, looked for all the world like a youngish priest, a divinity student probing gently into some theological problem. Appearances could not have been more deceptive, for he was essentially a fighting man and nothing else. Part of his skull had been removed by a shell splinter in some colonial war, which may have explained a lot; he described himself as a '*tête brulée*', hot-headed, which no one who knew him would say was an understatement. I got to know him well in Africa and then in the Levant and became very fond of him, although he was often quite exasperating, and enjoyed nothing so much as thwarting the British authorities.

He first came within my purview a few weeks after de Gaulle's visit to Trentham Park when he and most of his men, having joined the Free French, had been shepherded to a camp in the Aldershot area. A complaint was sent in from the town to our local military authorities that some legionaires had run riot in the streets the night before and looted shops. The Deputy Adjutant General called up Maigrin Verneret on the telephone, lodging a firm and shocked protest and asking him to do something about it, and perhaps he would be kind enough to inform him of the steps he had taken. "Oh," said Maigrin Verneret, "I can tell you now. I have not been satisfied with the discipline of the Legion for some time, idleness does not suit them, they are rather out of hand. I shall shoot a couple tomorrow morning." The officer he spoke to was so taken aback as to become ungrammatical, as, in a strangled voice, he said, "But you can't do that there here", or words to that effect.

The result was the formulation by the government of a regulation applying to all Allied troops in England, allowing them to apply their own codes of discipline, but denying them the right to carry out the death penalty without the consent of the British military legal authorities.

The legionaires followed their colonel with complete faith, for they knew he embodied the spirit of the Legion. He was so much more a legionaire than a Frenchman that he made it clear nationality was a minor question in his beloved corps, for he boasted he was first and foremost a citizen of the Franche-Comté, barely a Frenchman since his province had only become part of France, as recently as 1678, by the Treaty of Nijmwegen. I do not think he would have fought French troops from choice, but the abomination of abominations to him would be that the Legion should fight the Legion. When in the Syrian campaign Legion battalions on the Vichy side appeared facing the Free French legionaires Maigrin Verneret withdrew to his tents.

Over the years generations of French officers of the Legion can claim the credit of having formed one of the greatest fighting formations the world has ever known. Their pay was too small to be an inducement, so it was the leadership of their officers that had welded these men of many nations, who had enlisted for many different reasons, into such magnificent units that they placed love of the Legion above that of life itself. In the latter part of the first war when the distinction of '*fourragères*' was given to units for specially gallant conduct under fire, it was difficult to ensure that the Legion did not outpace the whole French army. There were many Germans in their ranks, but de Gaulle always maintained they were mostly French. I only know that in the 1914 war the Germans among them were sent to serve in Morocco.

A major obstacle to de Gaulle's efforts to obtain recruits were the activities of the Vichy officials in England. Chartier, the French Consul General in London, and the consuls in other cities, had been allowed to remain and to carry on with their functions unimpeded. These consuls sent emissaries in every direction to contact de Gaulle's recruits, told them they were traitors to their country, that they were joining a rebel who had been condemned to death by the legal government of France and would therefore be rebels themselves, that their families would suffer in consequence, but that they could be instantly released from an engagement which had no validity and would then soon be returned to France which was no longer at war. These arguments, especially the last, were generally effective, and de Gaulle's forces did not grow.

The difficult sport of running with the hare and hunting with the hounds had patrons in the Foreign Office and in other departments. The miasmic clouds of Munich defeatism and pusillanimity still lingered and clung to many desks in Whitehall. I personally fought and fought this attitude, sometimes very roughly, making many enemies as I went. I believed that such policies should be combated and exposed, for I was convinced that the kind of war we were engaged in could not be won by half measures or by appeasing half enemies. This was of course the prime minister's point of view, but he could not pursue every defeatist trail to its source. He had more things to do than to argue with cabinet colleagues and others who urged that if Pétain were not propitiated and humoured he would join the Nazis. I do not think that even Churchill ever succeeded in completely reducing to silence those who believed one could, if not win a war, at least not lose it, by carefully refraining from hitting hard in the hope of avoiding being hit in return.

In our relations with de Gaulle a case involving our own good faith was soon to arise. I did not hear what had occurred for some time and never discussed it with him, it was too shaming, but he heard about it too.

As has been seen, Frenchmen joining de Gaulle were to be given all the advantages to which an Englishman was entitled. I had been present at the meeting when this had been settled between de Gaulle and the Prime Minister.

I was also present at another interview in the Cabinet Room of No. 10 Downing Street between these two. The only other person present was General Dill, the Chief of the Imperial General Staff. The undertaking to French volunteers was confirmed and some further points put forward by de Gaulle were conceded by the Prime Minister.

De Gaulle then broached a question of vital importance to him: that of being given permission to recruit among the French troops in camps in England who were to be allowed to return to France if they opted to do so.

De Gaulle argued, and I supported him, that these Frenchmen should at least be given the choice of fighting on at our side, and that they should be told of the conditions under which they could do so.

General Dill expressed the fear that this might lead to unrest among the French troops. We could not contemplate any risk of disorders. True enough. But why should such an announcement have this effect? countered de Gaulle. He did not ask for leave to harangue the troops, it was merely a question of informing them of the situation. It would surely be wrong if some soldiers, anxious to go on with the war, found, having returned to France, that they might have done so had they known.

Although the idea evidently did not appeal to the CIGS, the

prime minister granted de Gaulle's request. The question next arose as to who was to visit the camps and publish the information. De Gaulle had too few officers to do so. I argued that as this was a British offer it should be put forward by British officers. This being accepted, I offered to provide these, as I had by then sufficient personnel for the purpose. I was surprised that the CIGS insisted that the message should be conveyed by officers from the War Office, but saw no reason why I should not agree.

It was only much later that I heard what had happened from some of those who carried out this duty. They had gone to the camps, and, standing on a table, chair or box, had addressed the French officers. They read the official message sanctioned by the Prime Minister giving the terms of service. Having done this, they descended from their pedestals and added, as they had been instructed to do, presumably by the War Office: "This is the official message we have been ordered to give you, But having done so we would like to add that we hope you will elect to return to France!" There can be no cause for astonishment that, faced with so chilling an invitation, few responded. Meanwhile, entirely ignorant of this, I grieved, as no doubt de Gaulle did, at the lack of response of the French.

When, long afterwards, I heard the explanation I choked with indignation at so flagrant a disregard of the spirit of the prime minister's instructions. It was not till much later still that I, in turn, understood the attitude of the War Office and had to admit that it had some justification, though there was none for the blatant disregard of the Prime Minister's orders.

True, the French had their rifles but no reserves of ammunition, so that we, who were so desperately in need of weapons for our own men who were longing for the opportunity to fight for their country, would have to deprive some of them of this privilege for the sake of arming foreigners whose fighting qualities had proved so dubious in defence of their own land. Those even in high and responsible places could not be expected to differentiate between the French units that had fought magnificently and those that had not, nor could they appreciate that in the straits we were then in volunteers prepared to continue the fight from England could not but be splendid material. All the military leaders could see was England's deadly peril and the obvious fact that her defence was best left in British hands. They could not tolerate the thought of breaches in our lines such as had occurred in France. It would perhaps have been too much to expect our commanding officers, overburdened by responsibilities, to understand the prime minister's reasons even had they known them.

But all this opposition, by underhand and indirect methods, must have been heartbreaking to the man who had placed his fate and, as he believed, that of France, in the hands of a country which must have seemed to him to contain few among her leaders who were completely dependable, apart from the Prime Minister.

Time and time again what were well-meant efforts on the part of many to express sympathy and extend hospitality to the French were thwarted either by red tape, or sometimes by perfectly genuine security requirements, oftener still by sheer stupidity. Public relations were unknown country to the official world, a deficiency which the members of my mission did their best to remedy. But it was a huge problem.

For instance, the White City and Olympia were allocated to the French troops and refugee civilians. Immense pains were taken and much devotion was shown by British volunteers in looking after them, starting canteens, etc. The government provided civilian clothes for those who needed them. But to these lonely men stranded on a foreign shore by the upheaval that had destroyed their country, the fact that security demanded that they should accept control checks and return by given times to their centres had the effect on lacerated pride of making them feel they were prisoners and not guests in England. A visit by the king and queen was sourly appreciated, no more.

De Gaulle paid his refugee compatriots a visit. It was a dismal failure. Then and later he showed himself utterly unable to make contact with his audience. His speech was received in dead silence. Nor did he succeed in conveying a human touch when he reviewed

the men. The difference between de Gaulle then and now is very
noteworthy. Today, careful tuition and practice have enabled
him to express a geniality which was perhaps always there but
which in 1940 lay as unfathomably deep and lost as Atlantis.
To the unhappy compatriots he reviewed he seemed as flexible as
the obelisk on the Place de la Concorde, as welcoming as the
hindquarters of a *guards municipal* horse.

Was it shyness assuming the stiff unbending guise of haughti-
ness? Perhaps. If he analysed the reason for his deficiency he was
unable to remedy it. Later I saw him review troops in Africa
when he did me the honour of asking me to accompany him.
He never seemed to be able to unbend. He gave the impression
of being implacable, which indeed he was. This was perhaps one
of his strengths. In England I only accompanied him when the
king reviewed his small forces at Aldershot. It would not have
done to give the impression he had a British bear-leader, which
was certainly not the case.

That the British were unresponsive and lacking in understanding must have been no cause of surprise to de Gaulle, who expected little else in spite of his English grandmother; but what
must have been terribly wounding was the bitter antagonism so
often displayed by his own countrymen.

If there were well-wishers amongst the French officials, including those in England, they did not express their sympathy. "The
legitimate government of France"; "We must be loyal to the
marshal"; "*de Gaulle, c'est la dissidence*", were phrases which were
audible amongst them, while seldom mentioned but at least as
potent were other motives – fear of loss of pension, liability to
punishment, forfeiture of property, and, strongest of all, anxiety
for their families in occupied France.

There were, of course, a minority of very brave Frenchmen
whom no personal considerations deflected from the urge to
fight on for France. They included a few lads who escaped from
the French coast in tiny fishing boats, and one remarkable young
man who flew over in an aeroplane he had built himself.

For the rest, only a few newly arrived from France or from

foreign countries and a solid nucleus of the French colony in England, people who had made their lives amongst us, rallied to de Gaulle.

Senior officers who rallied were very few, and their motives were not always purely patriotic – General Catroux, Governor General of Indo-China, for example, who, having been dismissed by the Vichy government for his policy of placating the Japanese, which exceeded even what the Vichy government could tolerate, approached the British government before committing himself to de Gaulle for assurances that he would receive from the British the pay and privileges to which he considered his rank entitled him.

3

In those first weeks after de Gaulle's arrival in England he had little to encourage him and much to endure. But neither the occasional tactlessness of the English nor the lack of response from his compatriots was the worst trial he had to endure. I have no doubt that his greatest ordeal was Oran – the destruction by a British fleet of the proudest ships in the French navy, which were assembled in the great French naval base of Mers-el-Kebir in Algeria.

The fate of the French fleet was one of our government's major preoccupations. Should it fall into German hands the result would be catastrophic.

I do not think that at this period of the war anyone believed that Admiral Darlan would willingly allow the French fleet to be taken over by the Germans and used against us. I certainly did not, but what I did believe was that the moment it suited the Germans they could, if these ships remained under French control, bring such pressure on the French government and the captive French nation as to compel their surrender.

I had developed this theme with the Prime Minister from the day I had returned from Bordeaux. The Germans were completely ruthless and would, I was convinced, stop at nothing to gain their ends. They might well announce that the fleet must be surrendered by a given day, failing which they would burn down a great town for every day's delay, Bordeaux on Monday, Lyons on Tuesday, Nantes on Wednesday and finally Paris on Saturday. In fact the question of the French fleet stood at the very forefront of British preoccupations at the beginning of July, as it had ever since France had shown signs of collapsing. Something had to be done, and the British government took the very grave decision that, at all costs, the French ships must be prevented from being used by the Germans against us.

On the afternoon of the 2nd July, 1940, the Prime Minister sent for me to No. 10 Downing Street. I was in the dentist's chair when I received the summons. He handed me the ultimatum Admiral Somerville[1] was to deliver to the French Admiral Gensoul, commanding the French fleet at Oran, next day. This was as follows:

> It is impossible for us, your comrades up to now, to allow your fine ships to fall into the power of the German or Italian enemy. We are determined to fight on to the end, and if we win, as we think we shall, we shall never forget that France was our Ally, that our interests are the same as hers, and that our common enemy is Germany. Should we conquer, we solemnly declare that we shall restore the greatness and territory of France. For this purpose, we must make sure that the best ships of the French Navy are not used against us by the common foe. In these circumstances His Majesty's Government have instructed me to demand that the French Fleet now at Mers-el-Kebir and Oran shall act in accordance with one of the following alternatives:

[1] Commander of 'Force H' based on Gibraltar. This consisted of the battle-cruiser *Hood*, the battleships *Valiant* and *Resolution*, the *Ark Royal*, two cruisers and eleven destroyers.

(a) Sail with us and continue to fight for victory against the Germans and Italians.

(b) Sail with reduced crews under our control to a British port. The reduced crews will be repatriated at the earliest moment.

If either of these courses is adopted by you, we will restore your ships to France at the conclusion of the war or pay full compensation, if they are damaged meanwhile.

(c) Alternatively, if you feel bound to stipulate that your ships should not be used against the Germans or Italians unless these break the Armistice, then sail them with us with reduced crews to some French port in the West Indies – Martinique, for instance – where they can be demilitarised to our satisfaction, or perhaps be entrusted to the United States and remain safe until the end of the war, the crews being repatriated.

If you refuse these fair offers, I must, with profound regret, require you to sink your ships within six hours.

Finally, failing the above, I have the orders of His Majesty's Government to use what ever force may be necessary to prevent your ships from falling into German or Italian hands.

It was a painful document to read as it had undoubtedly been for the Prime Minister to draft. Fortunately it was not the kind of document a man was likely to have to read more than once in a lifetime.

In itself it seemed to me that it could not have stated the case better or more fairly, in view of the rigour of our own inexorable situation.

"Do you think Gensoul will accept?" said Churchill. "I think he is bound to if he is made to realise we mean what we say." In which I was wrong, but I cannot regret that Admiral Somerville showed extreme reluctance, indeed horror, at the prospect of having to carry out his instructions should the ultimatum be refused.

"When can I tell de Gaulle? He must be informed before the ultimatum is delivered."

"Not today," said the Prime Minister. I was glad de Gaulle had not been involved in the decision, which was for us alone to take, one dictated solely by our own interests.

I left, dragging my feet, weighed down by the knowledge that so many years of my childhood spent in France were now dead, for they could never again be evoked happily.

That evening, driving myself home as usual through Hyde Park, I came across a band of French sailors running about and 'rough housing' with an equal number of English girls, of the type that always seems to be available to take kindly to foreign military men of any nationality. For wit, conversation and a common language, the girls substituted discordant squeals punctuated by high screeches and giggles as they dodged the laughing sailors with the red pompon-tipped caps in close pursuit of them.

But I was seeing other sailors, the same as these, on battleships in a distant African harbour, strolling about the decks or looking at the sea, the same sea that bathed the shores of many of their villages, no doubt wondering when they could go home. In all probability some of them were saying to one another that, as France was now out of the war, there was no justification for keeping them in these hot battleships when it was so cool at home. Everything was lovely at home.

There were few cars about that evening, which was probably fortunate, and I did not hit anything, although I could not see very clearly, for I had become suddenly convinced that in spite of all reason and common sense the adventure at Oran would end in tragedy.

Next day I told de Gaulle of the ultimatum. A man of few words, he seldom wasted them to comment on the inevitable, only moving his head slightly from side to side when forming a sentence of great importance which he might or might not utter. For a moment he was silent, but presently he said that he thought Gensoul would accept one of the alternatives offered him.

I spent the long afternoon when the ultimatum was being delivered at the committee dealing with French affairs at Gwydyr

House presided over by Desmond Morton, on which nearly every department of state was represented. We were kept informed almost hourly by the admiral representing the Admiralty as to what was going on at Oran. Admiral Somerville's hesitations were understandable but exasperating, for it seemed at one time as if Gensoul, obviously playing for time, would succeed by his tergiversations in reaching the goal of darkness, when his ships could escape to French harbours, that is to ultimate German control, which some of them in fact did.

I had a picture in my mind of the officer charged with the duty of delivering the ultimatum, Captain Holland RN, who had been Naval Attaché in Paris and whom I knew. He was devoted to the French, and it was right that an officer so well known and so well liked by them should endeavour to induce them to appreciate the force of the proposals and how well meant they were. But I knew as the afternoon wore on that Holland must have felt as if he had been put in charge of a firing squad and ordered to shoot his best friend.

After negotiating all day, Admiral Somerville, in accordance with his instructions, opened fire at 5.54 pm. After a bombardment lasting ten minutes, followed by heavy attacks by naval aircraft, the battleship *Bretagne* blew up, the *Dunkerque* ran aground and the *Provence* was beached. Only the *Strasbourg* escaped, though damaged by torpedo aircraft. Later that night some of my feelings of horror and despair at what had happened thanks to Gensoul's obstinacy and, no doubt, to the orders he had received, were mitigated when I learnt that he had sent messages to the Italian fleet (no doubt via the French Admiralty) asking it to attack our ships in the rear while he kept us in play.

That evening I saw de Gaulle again. His calmness was very striking, the objectivity of his view astonishing. He had evidently done a lot of thinking. What we had done, he said, was no doubt inevitable from our point of view. Yes, it was inevitable, but what he had to decide was whether he could still collaborate with us or whether he would retire from the scene and withdraw to private life in Canada. He had not yet made up his mind but would do so before morning. I only said that the cause of France remained. She still had to be saved. Those Frenchmen who wished to fight on, and their numbers were growing, required a leader, and he was the only one.

I then went to tell the Prime Minister of the magnificent dignity displayed by de Gaulle.

Next day de Gaulle told me he had decided that he would remain in the war at our side.

This decision went beyond heroism, it was that of a man prepared to face martyrdom for the sake of his country.

His night's meditation had confirmed his conviction that to fight on at our side presented the only chance for France to survive as a great nation, but he knew that to collaborate with us after Oran meant offering himself in sacrifice to the hatred of his compatriots.

Duff Cooper had the intelligent comprehension to allow him to speak on the BBC on the 8th July without let or hindrance, judging rightly that though de Gaulle was certain to be very critical of British action at Oran he would also and inevitably explain, though it was impossible he should endorse, our point of view. This in fact was what he did.

He quite rightly castigated that section of our press which had inferred the operation was in some way a military victory, but finally concluded that it was inevitable that under the Armistice accepted by the Pétain government somehow, sometime, the French fleet would fall into German hands. And, he said, it was far better that France's magnificent ships should be wrecked at Mers-el-Kebir than one day be manned by German crews to attack Britain. A brave thing to say to a France overwhelmed with sorrow and resentment, whose ears were filled with the clamour of vituperation voiced by the Vichy government led by Admiral Darlan. What a strangely vain man he must have been to believe that his promise that the French fleet would never fall into German hands was either possible to fulfil or would be credible to us.

What happened at Bizerta in 1942 was the complete justification of the British action at Oran in 1940. On the 8th December in that year the French Admiral Derrien, Naval Commander and Governor of Bizerta, was requested to meet at 9 pm the German General Gausse who handed him the following letter:

> The Führer has ordered that all the French troops in North Africa should be demobilised and transferred to France. Without having any personal suspicion concerning you, we cannot fight having French troops at our backs. I am instructed to request you to issue orders that all ships, batteries, wireless installations and arms be handed over intact to the German and Italian troops, and that your officers, NCO's and men be concentrated on a peninsula south of Bizerta. Any damage or sinking will be dealt with by court martial. Should you not be able to accept these conditions, and if any resistance is offered to the handing over of the ships, if they are either sunk or damaged, all the ships and batteries will be bombarded forthwith by shells and bombs of the heaviest calibre, and attacked by our troops until they are completely destroyed.
>
> The crews, down to the last officer and man, will be killed. No prisoners will be taken since after the dissolution of the French forces by Marshal Pétain your troops will no longer be considered to be regular by the laws of war.
>
> You, Admiral, must make the decision: either face return to France or death. Answer within thirty minutes and take the necessary dispositions within this time limit, failing which our action will start automatically.

The German forces required to carry out this ultimatum, aircraft, troops, ships, tanks had been ostentatiously deployed. At 10.30 am Admiral Derrien sent out the message: "I had to accept this 'Diktat'. The troops of the Axis have taken all measures to repress by force and without pity any attempt at resistance, sabotage or sinking. I request all to obey."

4

In the early morning of the 3rd July, on the same day that the ultimatum was delivered to Admiral Gensoul at Oran, all the French vessels at Portsmouth and Plymouth were invaded by British troops and marines and the officers taken ashore under armed escort. The officers later complained bitterly that their cabins had been pillaged.

This action was no doubt necessary for two reasons: because of what might happen as a result of the action at Oran, and also because of Darlan's order to the ships in British waters to sail for French North African harbours. The British Admiralty was aware of this order. It was not at all impossible, such was the mentality of the French naval officers and their veneration of Darlan, that they might attempt to shoot their way out, which would have been a fearful disaster. Necessary though it no doubt was, however, I have always felt that the way the operation was carried out was inexcusable. It justified the resentment aroused amongst the French officers and men.

The ships' companies were interned at Aintree, near Liverpool, under circumstances lacking comfort and dignity. There were between ten and fifteen thousand of them and they lived in tents under conditions of considerable discomfort, which would have been normal enough to British conscripts but was hard on men used to a less harsh climate and to living in ships.

The ratings, although in reality very much under the control of their officers, who did not, however, choose to exercise discipline over them in matters unconnected with their own affairs, wandered about Liverpool at will, refused to make payment for such things as bus or tram fares, and filled the citizens, deprived by the call-up of much of their normal protection, with considerable apprehension.

It had occurred to the local military to offer them an extra 6d a day as pay, a considerable sum in those days, if they would help dig the trenches we stood in such need of and which we simply did not have the manpower to excavate ourselves. A very few accepted, but later refused, as did all the others, claiming that France was now out of the war and that to do this work would be an unneutral act. They ceaselessly demanded to be sent back to France.

On reports that his few and unimpressive representatives were having little or no response to their pleas to the sailors that they should join him, de Gaulle decided to go to Liverpool himself. He was met with overt hostility from men who constantly listened on the wireless to every word put out by the Vichy government. His naval deputy, Admiral Muselier, fared no better at their hands. This sailor, who looked like a Marseilles pirate, had joined the Free French more out of hatred for Darlan, who had a poor opinion of him, than for love of the Free French cause. He was detested by his colleagues in the French navy. At one moment we put him in gaol, quite unjustifiably, but presently the Royal Navy took him to its heart, owing to the extremely strong international admirals' trade union, a fundamental rule of which appears to be that any admiral of whatever nationality is, without cavil or discussion, of a superior essence to any soldier or civilian.

It was under these circumstances that I offered to go to Liverpool and speak to the French sailors. I did so two or three times. I knew it would be difficult and unpleasant, but thought that, perhaps, as de Gaulle and his people had been so unsuccessful, the men might listen to a friendly Englishman whose sole object was to offer them the glorious possibility of joining Britain in the liberation of France. In any case I thought it my duty to try. I did not realise the depth of the bitter resentment they felt at the harsh manner in which they had been evicted from their ships. This had understandably left the impression of bad faith in their minds. Our offer of service in the British navy to technicians we were short of was taken by the officers (and de Gaulle) to be an attempt to disrupt their crews by enticing into our service invaluable naval specialists of whom we stood in great need. Indeed this may have been the purpose of some junior British officers.

De Gaulle wished me luck as I went. Flying in a small machine, I had the unpleasant experience half way to my destination of finding myself in the midst of many aeroplanes. I thought this must be a hostile raid, but they turned out to be British and vanished as suddenly as they had appeared.

The start of my venture was not auspicious. The Royal Navy had very thoughtfully put out loud speakers so that I could address the great concourse of men, but the French had cut the leads, having no idea of what these preparations purported. I found the camp surrounded by barbed wire, and British soldiers posted round it to prevent the sailors breaking out by other than the authorised exits.

The officer in charge turned out to be a young colleague of mine in the House of Commons.

He said the French sailors pelted his sentries with lumps of earth or stones and that he had the greatest difficulty in preventing them shooting in retaliation.

I walked into the camp completely alone, politics having taught me the advantage a single man possesses when addressing a large audience.

It was a Sunday morning and the entire camp was at Mass. Meeting a petty officer I asked him to convey my compliments to the senior officer and to say I should be glad to be given the opportunity of addressing the officers as soon as possible after Mass and when could I do so? Presently an officer appeared and suggested as a meeting place a large room under the stands.

Some three hundred officers were soon collected, the seniors in front. The admirals sitting on chairs in solitary state were in the van.

Although I disapproved utterly of the way in which these men had been taken from their ships, I did not apologise, dwelling on our difficulties and dangers which must excuse many of our shortcomings. If our guests were uncomfortable so were we. I begged my audience to remember that we were alone in opposing Nazi Germany, but determined whatever happened to fight on to the last with the complete faith that somehow, someday, in God's good time, we would win, and that our victory would also be that of France. As this was my absolute belief it was not difficult to find words to express it. But never have I addressed so implacably hostile an audience, or so it seemed. I learnt later that there were some sympathisers among them, but on this occasion, under the eyes of the admirals, they were silent.

The officers were, however, correct, only interrupting me whenever I said "government of Vichy", with the cry "the government of France".

There were at the end of my speech some justifiable complaints concerning conditions in the camp, which I promised to have remedied, but it was quite evident from the attitude of the admirals, and to a lesser degree that of other senior officers, that so long as they were in contact with their men they would prevent any of them joining de Gaulle. So obvious was this that by telephone from Aintree I asked for and obtained that the admirals be invited to go to more congenial quarters. They were sent to Oxford, I think. A suggestion I made that the senior officers be sent to comfortable lodgings in another town was accepted. Only a few who were reported to be actively hostile were sent to another camp. The remainder were divided by ships' companies and sent to different camps. These I subsequently addressed, speaking direct to the men in the presence of their officers.

These young, healthy sailors filled me with real despair for France. They only cared about returning home. That they would place their necks under the German boot seemed to matter to them not at all. Nothing would induce them to fight on our side under de Gaulle. The fact that we were fighting on caused them neither shame nor envy. That was our business and of no interest to them. The war was over as far as they were concerned. All they wanted was to go home – home – home; furthermore, they did not like camping in so cold a climate. On one occasion, exasperated by such remarks, I said that the climate bred the airmen who were striking hard at the enemy that very day, and perhaps a stay under our inclement skies might not turn out to be bad for them or for France.

Some officers asked to see me privately and spoke of real hardships they had undergone. A few came to see me in London. Among them were men whom it was a pleasure to help and whom I would have been honoured to consider friends for life.

Only in one camp did an officer display such evidence of hostility that I had him transferred there and then.

But these talks and those given by the very few Free French officers available must have done some good, for presently some officers and men did join the Free French. Admiral Muselier also reported some success.

Unfortunately we were fated, in spite of really good intentions, to thwart and offend the French.

When the *Meknes*, loaded with Frenchmen who had opted to return to France, was sunk by the Germans in spite of the illuminated Tricolour painted on deck and of the warning of its passage they had been given, the Germans promptly proclaimed it was we who had sunk the ship, and there were Frenchmen who believed this. There were many lost but also many survivors. The Admiralty provided entirely new outfits for those brought ashore, but they were treated by the military authorities as prisoners; armed sentries were stationed in the corridors of the trains conveying them north. They were not allowed to get out onto the platforms at stations in search of water which was not provided on the train. This barbarous manifestation of bad manners and cruel inhospitality naturally caused great bitterness and resentment.

The arrangements for the embarkation of the French sailors for France, suggested by the pro-Vichy authorities still in England and accepted by us, were a bitter pill for de Gaulle, for they turned the choice the Prime Minister had decided they should be allowed to make between fighting with de Gaulle or returning to France into a farce. A young Free French warrant officer put them the question "Do you wish to remain and fight under General de Gaulle" at the quayside under the scrutiny of two of their own pro-Vichy officers, who made no bones about ordering or pushing the men onto the ship's gangway.

Even more ridiculous was the embarkation of the majority of the troops who had opted to return to France.

I had strongly argued that they should leave their weapons behind them. Why, I said, send these back to France under German occupation? Who could say that they would not be turned against us one day? All too true a forecast of what was to happen in Syria and North Africa. But General Dill and other military authorities would have none of it. The soldiers would consider themselves dishonoured if their sidearms and weapons were taken from them; the Frenchmen, so touchy in matters of honour, would resist, there would be riots – and the bugbear of having to deal with French soldiers in revolt was evoked as it had been before.

The War Office had its way and ship after ship (which contrary to undertakings given by the Vichy government failed to return) was loaded with Frenchmen who all turned up at the quayside not only with rifles and bayonets but with the excellent small tanks which were part of a battalion's equipment. The trouble was that the embarkation officers had not been told of the ticklish point of honour involved in bidding a French soldier divest himself of his weapons. Concerned only with logistics, they bade the soldiers, as they left the trains, throw their rifles on one heap and their bayonets on another, which of course they did without demur.

Then British fatigue parties loaded all these weapons, together with the tanks which would have been so useful to us, on another ship which followed after those loaded with the men. It would have been tragic if it had not been so silly. General de Gaulle did no more than shrug his shoulders and say: "Will they never learn?"

He had meanwhile won a notable victory over us in another field. Our intelligence services were anxious to drop Frenchmen in France who would send back information on an immense variety of subjects, notably and most important of all, lists of well-disposed French men and women; for though France had been our ally and indeed because she had been our ally we had little useful information concerning her for our present purposes.

None of our intelligence services had worked in France. We relied on the French for all intelligence concerning their own country. I well remember saying I would pledge the government to pay a million pounds for a reliable list of well wishers all over France. It would have been cheap at the price.

But de Gaulle flatly refused to allow any Frenchmen under his control to be dropped in France unless he was consulted and informed of their mission.

Having recognised him, it was impossible to seek Frenchmen outside his authority to do the job, and he was adamant. Ismay[1] failed to move him, so we finally gave way, breaking with every principle of intelligence security.

On this question of controlling all Frenchmen de Gaulle was inflexible. He proved to be apt, as are all his countrymen, at twisting agreements we had signed, to cover cases unforeseen when they were made.

There was in particular the case of a number of French aviators who, at the time of France's collapse, joined the British air force and wore our uniform. De Gaulle insisted they should be compelled to join the Free French. This of course we could not make them do, but they were informed of de Gaulle's views. Later, in Egypt, I participated in most painful interviews between de Gaulle and Air Marshal Tedder when the general demanded that those Frenchmen who had served the common cause well and loyally and who refused to join the Free French should be forced to do so. In vain was it argued that we had an engagement of honour with these men. His answer was that if they landed in territories controlled by him he would have them shot as deserters. But this was the ultra de Gaulle, the one who sometimes flew into blind rages and on one occasion gave a month's fortress arrest (he had no fortress but it was awkward all the same) to the excellent and devoted Colonel des Essarts for the crime of going to bid farewell to General Wavell, whose liaison officer des Essarts had been and who was greatly attached to him, on Wavell's departure for India. We had had sporadic manifestations of the same kind in

[1] General Lord Ismay, Chief of Staff to Sir Winston Churchill.

England. On two occasions de Gaulle had consigned officers to the Tower without the least authority for doing so. On the first occasion the problem this act of authority presented was easily resolved without its becoming necessary to remind de Gaulle that we no longer lived in Tudor times, and that it was as un- usual to confine a person to the Tower without trial as it was to have him stretched on the rack. The prisoner, escorted in a taxi by a Colonel Brosset, simply opened the door of the taxi at the first red lights in Whitehall and stepped out. His escort, abashed but no doubt relieved at this solution, for he did not know enough English to call a policeman and would have been greatly em- barrassed had he had to explain his predicament even through an interpreter, shrugged his shoulders and, showing his address typed on a paper, was driven back to Carlton Gardens.

In the second case I heard of what was afoot in time and the officers of the company on duty in the Tower were kind enough to welcome the bewildered prisoner for long enough to enable us to convey to the head of the Free French that neither the use of the dungeons nor the services of the executioner were among the amenities we were prepared to place at his disposal.

5

As the whole of North Africa was closing ever more tightly with bared teeth and snarling ill will against de Gaulle, it was natural that many eyes should turn to the French colonies farther south – French Equatorial Africa, the Cameroons, Senegal and Gabon. It occurred to many that to rally these territories, which were interspersed between British ones on which they largely depended for trade and communications, might be an easier proposition than the strongly held Arab lands.

It was from there too that de Gaulle received indications that the spirit of resistance was more alive than elsewhere. Vichy was more remote, the civilian elements more powerful and vocal than in military-dominated and official-swamped North Africa. And Frenchmen in West Africa were fully aware and understandably apprehensive of what their fate would be if their commercial ties and their connections with the outside world were severed by a break with the British colonies, with which they had common business interests and in many cases administered regions composed of the same tribes.

De Gaulle naturally felt that there was every advantage in the French West African colonies rallying together, as there were dangers in their not doing so. Against a colony rallying singly, Vichy could still concentrate very considerable forces, naval, air and military, collected from African bases such as Casablanca and Dakar, not to mention those which might be sent from France, possibly with German connivance if not direct support or direction. De Gaulle by now knew enough of the British attitude to realise that such a situation would cause the utmost dismay in London and strengthen all those elements which, if not inimical, were at least lacking in sympathy for the Free French movement.

I was even more aware of this danger than he was, and was therefore in full sympathy with his plan to try to get all the West African colonies to rally together, creating a situation beyond Vichy's capacities to cope with and of such a moral strength as to drown the squawks of those who felt it ill mannered and undiplomatic to cross old Marshal Pétain's dream of a penitent France expiating all her past sins by placing her neck under the German boot, and proving her determination never to sin again by surrendering her freedom and her free will for ever by accepting the status of slaves to the Nazis, who would henceforth dispose of her body and soul. Such surrenders have been one way of avoiding responsibility since the world began.

Lord Lloyd, the Colonial Secretary, was also an enthusiastic proponent of the policy of rallying the French West African colonies to de Gaulle, and sent instructions to the British colonial governors to give all possible support to his plans.

The first of the West African leaders to rally was Félix Eboué, the Negro governor of the Chad. I came to know him well a few months later, and he remains in my memory as one of the most distinguished men I have ever met. One of the things I remember best about him was his beautiful French, a language it is always pleasant to hear well spoken. He was no doubt deeply devoted to France, whose culture he had so well absorbed, but, so infinite are the facets of the human mind, so countless the number of its recesses, that it could never be asserted that something of the apprehension caused by the Nazi racial doctrine did not play some part in his attitude.

But the man on whom de Gaulle relied most to knit together the Free French movement in West Africa was Colonel de Larminat, probably the most distinguished early adherent to his movement.

De Larminat was professionally qualified and a man of high spirit and high principles.

He had been chief of staff to General Mittelhauser, the French commander in the Levant at the time of the Armistice, and had ardently supported his chief when the latter at first announced his rejection of it, but repudiated him when he later accepted it. De Larminat organised an exodus towards Palestine of Frenchmen determined to fight on, but was thwarted in this by Mittelhauser, whose action was favoured by the British military command in Cairo, hypnotised by the dread of hordes of Pétainist Frenchmen creating yet one more threat to security that our overstretched forces would be unable to deal with. De Larminat's bellicosity lead to his being arrested, but he escaped and made his way to Cairo and was on a ship bound for England via the Cape when the British authorities intercepted him at Durban with a message from de Gaulle asking him to proceed to Leopoldville, the capital of the Belgian Congo, by air, where he was to be given the mission of rallying French Equatorial Africa, in whose capital, Brazzaville, he had great influence.

De Larminat's strong personality was on subsequent occasions to lead to difficulties with the British command, whose directions he would only accept in the most general terms. He was a well-bred man of excellent, if rather distant, and perhaps saturnine manners and was a true representative of the Auvergne mountains of central France from whence he hailed. His very features bore the stamp of that rather special people.

He was completely military and so much identified with his profession as never to wear anything but walking shoes indoors, apparently ready to obey marching orders at any moment. I do not think he owned a pair of slippers. He was a man of complete military loyalty in all its rugged simplicity. Having accepted de Gaulle as his leader he never deviated from that obedience, and de Gaulle never failed to take full advantage of it. No one will perhaps ever know what occurred when in June 1962 the court martial set up by de Gaulle acquitted General Salan, and de Gaulle appointed de Larminat president of the military court to try Salan once more. All that is known is that de Larminat blew out his brains rather than discharge this mission.

The rallying of the French colonies was synchronised at Lagos with the benevolent acquiescence of Sir Bernard Bourdillon, Governor-General of Nigeria.

I obtained from the Prime Minister[1] the use of one of our very rare flying boats to take de Gaulle's emissaries on their hazardous mission, and one day early in August there set out in it a tiny posse of good Frenchmen, de Boislambert: a small man with a heart so big you wondered it could be contained in his short frame, extremely brave, perfectly loyal and very intelligent; Commandant Leclerc de Hauteclocque, a regular cavalry officer, to become very well known as Leclerc; and Pleven, who was to make a brilliant political career under de Gaulle.

It was good to see Pleven in London all martial ardour, for when I had met him in Paris in the bad days of defeat it was difficult to imagine his tears would ever dry up. Indeed, no one could blame a Frenchman for weeping in those days.

And there was also the very gallant, the excellent Commandant Parant.

[1] De Gaulle in his Memoirs, page 92, says this was given him by Lord Lloyd. This was not so. These aircraft were not in his control.

M

Leclerc was a good type of cavalry officer, typical of that arm, and might just as well have been British, excepting that he was rather more animated than you would have expected an Englishman to be. He was light-hearted and light in body, gay in a serious sort of way, with a fair but not excessive sense of humour. He was a gentleman and owned a property just north of Amiens.

His adventures at the time of the collapse of France were typical of the man, his coolness and his luck. He escaped from the German net, which embraced the whole French army, and made for his house, which he found full of Austrian soldiers. One of them was riding his wife's bicycle round the house. He gave him a severe scolding for taking property that was not his and threatened to accuse him of looting, announcing that this was his house. The cowed soldier slunk away, and Leclerc went upstairs and put on a civilian suit, came down and rode off on his wife's bicycle all the way to Bordeaux.

There, most extraordinary of all, he at once ran into his wife. He asked her if she had any money. She happened to have drawn all the family's available funds, some twenty thousand francs, I think, which she handed to him, and he thereupon took steps to get to England.

What is wholly admirable and quite characteristic was that he never hesitated for a moment to go on fighting.

From Lagos he and Boislambert, encouraged by some British elements while others turned a blind eye, proceeded on what should be regarded as one of the boldest operations in history, the rallying of the French Cameroons. They were getting on with their plans quite well, it seemed, when General Giffard, the general commanding the British Forces in West Africa, got wind of the projected coup. Zeus in his wrath can hardly have issued more thunderbolts on learning of one of Mercury's worst pranks, and the GOC's rumblings were audible in London. These Frenchmen must be stopped at all costs, he commanded, or the whole of the Cameroons supported by every other French colony would attack his inadequate British forces. If this were allowed to happen would London send him the reinforcements he would then need?

He warned the civilian governors of the fate awaiting them, and on every telegraph line, by every signal, issued the most positive, the most stringent orders that the mad enterprise of these irresponsible Frenchmen must be stopped.

Meanwhile Boislambert and Leclerc, ignoring Giffard's protests and commands, slipped over to Victoria in the British Cameroons.

There, on the night of the 27th August, they, together with some twenty French sympathisers, embarked in three native canoes and made their way through the mangrove swamps, then by open sea, to the large harbour of Douala.

They were met as arranged by some sympathisers, made straight for the military headquarters, announcing to well-disposed listeners that they were taking over the colony in the name of de Gaulle. Those who were not co-operative were at once arrested. These new-type musketeers then proceeded to arrest the High Commissioner and others. In what now reads as a charming signal to de Gaulle they apologised for having assumed higher military rank than they were entitled to for the occasion.

Next day, having blocked the telegraph, they took the train up country to Yaoundé where most of the Vichy officials had collected.

They stopped at every station on the way announcing the colony had rallied to and been taken over by de Gaulle. Any objectors they took with them as prisoners. At Yaoundé they simply announced that Douala and the entire country between them and the capital had rallied. These statements, made with considerable firmness and aplomb, proved to be persuasive enough and few were those whose attitude required restrictive action.

Rather pathetically, these young, not so far very formidable conquistadors asked de Gaulle to send Free French naval and air forces and artillery, which were at this stage as imaginary as the land forces they so glibly invoked when talking to their Vichy opposite numbers. They must have realised this themselves, for the next day they sent a signal that they would be "grateful if a British warship could be sent to Douala", and, obligingly, His Majesty's Government sent HMS *Cumberland*.

I never knew General Giffard's reaction to this operation, nor did I ask him when I met him later. I have always assumed he must have considered it a shocking example of what terrible risks can be run by those who disregard the views of the authorities on the spot.

I was later, after the Dakar operation, to see something of Leclerc. He certainly grew with his increased responsibilities, and I have a pleasant memory of him in the Chad, where he was organising, on General de Gaulle's instructions, a remarkable march across the desert to the Fezzan oasis. Relaxed and pleasant, he took me to see two New Zealanders found by one of his patrolling armoured cars way out in the Sahara. They had marched an incredible distance in the sand after escaping from the Italians, with practically no water and, I remember, half a small jar of jam as their only food. What is very hard to forgive is that Italian cars came out to look at them in the distance day after day, and then left them still crawling to the south where they hoped freedom might lie. If Leclerc had never done more than show by voice and action his boundless admiration for the pluck of these men, and manifested it by his care of them, I for one would ever burn a candle to him in the shrine of my memory.

I never saw him again after this meeting in central Africa, but gave him then a very valuable Malacca cane I carried and told him with the kind of half second sight I sometimes have that as long as he had it with him he would come to no harm. Years later, after his death in North Africa in an air accident, an unknown person sent me a newspaper cutting telling the story of the cane, that he always carried it, looking on it as a talisman, but that, on that day, he had left it behind.

General de Gaulle announced to the world the rallying of the Chad Territory on the 27th August, 1940, which, with a fine touch of satire for the benefit of the non-belligerent Vichy, he described as the 360th day of the War. The Chad, rightly, was given the honour of rallying first. The Cameroons rallied the following day, and on the 28th August also de Larminat telegraphed to de Gaulle that he had arrived at Brazzaville and had assumed full powers. There had been no incidents.

On the 29th the Governor of the Gabon telegraphed his adherence to the Free French cause. The authorities at Dakar reacted quickly; and he announced he had made a mistake. A practice was thereupon initiated which was later perfected and extended in the Middle East. A naval hydroplane flew at frequent intervals from Dakar to Libreville, the capital of the Gabon, bringing orders to Vichy adherents and removing Free French sympathisers.

6

As the summer advanced and the bold initiatives of a handful of adventurous and brave Frenchmen were being planned and executed, a far more important move was being organised.

It is impossible to look at a map of West Africa without realising the importance of the French naval base of Dakar in Senegal, then strongly held by Vichy. It was powerfully defended, and was greatly strengthened by the fact that the *Richelieu*, the most heavily armed warship in the world, had taken refuge there.

It required no great strategic insight to appreciate the importance of Dakar. It was the nearest point in Africa to South America, and if the Germans could use it as a base, our Atlantic Ocean traffic would be greatly endangered, as would our communications with the British colonies on the West African coast, and with the Far East.

It may well be that General de Gaulle was, as he says, the first to suggest that an attempt should be made to capture the place. It is also true, as Churchill writes in Volume II of *The Second World War*, that "General de Gaulle, Major General Spears and Major Morton had evolved a plan in outline of which the object was to raise the Free French Flag in West Africa, to occupy Dakar and thus consolidate the French Colonies in West and Equatorial Africa for General de Gaulle".

De Gaulle had by then 7,000 men and it was important to consider where they could be best employed. When the idea of an attack on Dakar was first put up to the prime minister he countered by asking whether the best place for de Gaulle to land was not North Africa. It was not difficult to point out that under the conditions then prevailing this was impossible.

How did the idea of mastering Dakar develop?

As I had learnt in the First World War, to conceive a plan means little. Many a café strategist has elaborated great military conceptions illustrated with matches on marble tables. Several staff officers and French commanders had, to my knowledge, put forward as a possibility the manoeuvre that resulted in the victory of the Marne in 1914. Anyone knowing the position of the armies could have done so. It was obvious. But it could only be the man who assumed the responsibility, and faced the formidable risks involved, who could claim credit for the victory. This was General Joffre, the French commander-in-chief, who said later: "I do not know who won the battle of the Marne, but I know who would have been held responsible had it been lost." And it is Winston Churchill, the originator of the Dakar expedition, who is entitled to claim credit for a bold conception, although it failed through no fault of his.

The first plan put forward by de Gaulle was shown to be totally impracticable and was soon abandoned. He advocated landing a column at Konakri, miles south of Dakar, and attacking the place overland. No such march by a large military force across the African bush was possible. The time it would have taken would have enabled the Vichy forces to organise an overwhelming resistance, and they would no doubt have been pushed, coerced and possibly reinforced, against their will, by the Germans. It would also have been impossible to keep together for so long the British naval force required to cover such an expedition.

The plan eventually decided upon was for a joint British and Free French naval and military operation under British command.

Our preliminary meetings on Dakar at the Admiralty were held in the greatest secrecy, particular care being taken to conceal de Gaulle's presence there. In view of the incredible indiscretion displayed by some Free French officers these precautions seem in retrospect rather absurd. Once the general lines of the operation and its dates had been settled at meetings which de Gaulle and I attended with the joint commanders, Admiral Cunningham and General Irwin, neither I nor de Gaulle were kept in the picture beyond receiving the information necessary to enable de Gaulle to issue the necessary movement orders to his troops. Everything was in the hands of the planners.

When we entrained at Liverpool St. on the 30th August, a crate full of proclamations to the people of Dakar which burst open, scattering its contents on the station platform, gave a touch of the ridiculous to the cloak and dagger attitude to the enterprise.

My later impression when we reached our destination was one of astonishment at the little the navy knew about Dakar and its defences. Yet we had had a naval officer attached to the French staff there. Neither he nor the consular authorities seemed to have been very observant or to know the exact battery and gun emplacements. Nor did any one seem to know what weather conditions to expect. Fog was mentioned by no one.

We left Liverpool on the 1st September after a heavy German raid, and the thought of German submarines as our convoy zig-zagged its way through the very dangerous waters was most unpleasant.

De Gaulle and I embarked in the 16,000 ton Dutch liner *Westernland*. I have a still vivid picture of the gallant little Free French sloops keeping up with the great liners in heavy seas, of the intolerable heat in our ship, once the tropics were reached, with the lights masked and the air excluded.[1] I remember too the gay talk at the mess de Gaulle and I shared. Many of the French and British staffs were excellent raconteurs: I saw de Gaulle laugh then as I never did again. I shall never forget the French airman, Colonel Pijeaud, quoting from Pagnol's *Marius* in perfect Mar-

---

[1] The convoy consisted of the *Westernland* and the *Pennland*, carrying the French troops, the foodship *Belgravia*, and the *Karenja*. The *Sobieski*, the *Ettrick* and the *Kenya*, with the main British forces on board, sailed from Scapa Flow on the 31st August.

seillais – "*Stop – Stop – un peu plus vite que stop*" – and d'Argenlieu, whose urbanity concealed a will of iron.

Capitaine de Frégate d'Argenlieu, a professional naval officer, had joined the Carmelites, becoming a provincial of the order. He was one of the first to join de Gaulle and never wavered in his support of him. He knew and loved the Provençal poet Mistral and often discussed his gentle qualities on that long trip. It is probable that de Gaulle's ADC, de Courcel, was there too, he always was; but although omnipresent, he tended to fade into the landscape unperceived.

In 1941 de Gaulle, he and I crossed the Congo by night in a very uncomfortable one-engined Sabena plane and landed in the early morning at Juba in the British Sudan. So exiguous were British resources in those days that the small aerodrome was guarded by Belgian Congolese African soldiers, no doubt to re-lease better trained troops. We were met by a rather down-at-heels motor which looked like a taxi that had seen better days. De Gaulle and I sat in the back seat and de Courcel took his place on the occasional seat, the 'strapontin'. When we reached the entrance of the aerodrome the guard was turned out, evidently with the best of intentions, but it was not impressive as a military exercise. De Gaulle paid no attention. I glanced at him and returned the salute. De Courcel bent slightly forward and with a respectful touch of his knee as light as might have been that of a butterfly's wing said, "*Mon Général*, the guard is presenting arms to you." Whereupon de Gaulle volleyed these words at him: "I forbid you, do you hear, I forbid you ever to say anything like that again. I see everything, and if I did not return the salute of the guard it is because I did not wish to do so," and still he did not raise his hand to his cap.

I remembered this story when I heard later that de Courcel had asked to see active service in the desert. His request was granted, and he commanded an armoured car and was slightly wounded, after which, for a time at least, he resumed his vigilant wait, the servant of the tinkling bell.

De Gaulle and I often visited our Dutch Captain Piet Lageay, who commanded the *Westernland*. He was a remarkable person as a man and as a sailor. He was made of steel. He was not sure of the loyalty of all his officers, but ruled them with unobtrusive strength. An incipient mutiny among the stokers he dealt with by locking up the difficult ones at the very bottom of the ship under the engines, and there they remained in spite of justified panic and no doubt infernal conditions in submarine-infested waters. Indeed with deck after deck packed with men, it is difficult to see what chances of survival anyone would have had if the ship had been torpedoed. The blackout keeping out air as well as light made conditions intolerable in the tropical heat. There were very few electric fans on board and these had to be kept for the sick.

During those long days, watching the flying fish trying to preserve their miserable existence by darting out of the water to avoid an unseen assailant and plunging back quickly enough to avoid an ever-famished gull, I got to know some young French officers and was the better for listening to the unquenchable hope the unspent years distilled within them. I have forgotten even their names, but would still like to express my gratitude for the encouragement their faith in their own country gave me.

The troops on board, all Free French, were a strange assortment. There were some legionaires and many North Africans, and some of the entertainments they gave were excellent, but one gathered there were casualties most nights from knife fights, and I was very annoyed to fall flat outside my cabin over a corpse in the blackout one night. But probably the worst experience for the British on board, with our radio silenced, was to hear of the air attacks on London. What had really happened? What were the casualties? Did they include any of our families? We could not ask. But we were immensely cheered by the figures presently published of German air losses. "They cannot keep this up," said de Gaulle. "You have won."

Part of one of the decks had been set aside for de Gaulle and myself. Two armchairs had been provided. It would be unfair to try to remember all he said, naturally expecting that no confidence would be repeated or personal appreciations noted as he sat there for many an hour, often in silence, but de Gaulle did sometimes speak of his family, which he told me was the second oldest in Paris, having had a known residence there for over three hundred years. And on one occasion he said that when the war was over he would turn his back on public life in any form and withdraw to the country. "That is an illusion," I said. "You will find you simply cannot do so. There will always be something more to do, just one more step to take, the necessary consolidation of some measure not fully accepted or established, and there will be no one to take your place, no one you can be entirely sure will carry out the policy you have traced and which you will feel cannot be abandoned. No, *mon Général*, you have condemned yourself to a life sentence from which there is no reprieve."

I learnt from him something I have never forgotten, which is that men's real emotions are revealed by their hands, which they cannot control as they do their faces. I wondered later if this was why the sleeves of his tunic were very wide; he habitually thrust his hands into them after the manner of a monk. I believe one of his brothers was a monk.

It was during one of our sessions that I found he had the unusual but not very useful faculty of reading words backwards with great rapidity, a trick learnt as a solace from boredom; when going to the Lycée at Lille on top of a tram he used to read the names of the shops from tail to front.

He sometimes, not often, told stories against himself. For instance he told me of an incident when he was in command of a tank regiment at Metz. During a review a cavalry regiment was drawn up in line close in front of his machines. When he gave the order to start up the engines, there was an absolutely deafening noise under the horses' tails, which caused the terrified animals to indulge in a wild charge of their own on the reviewing general and the assembled guests. His description of this was very funny, as was his evocation of the fury of his superiors, which could be read in his expression more than gathered from his words.

He would look at large-scale maps for hours, and there can be no doubt he was practising his strategic imagination in evolving plans for the future development of the war. At that time, naturally, his attention was particularly concentrated on Africa.

Here is one example of how unusual and bold de Gaulle's imagination in military matters could be.

He developed to me in some detail a plan the object of which was to disrupt completely the German garrison in France with the object of compelling them to increase their troops in occupation there. A considerable number of specially trained motor cyclist signallers would be landed at a convenient point in northern or western France with, if possible, such light armoured cars as could be put ashore, and make at top speed for the Mediterranean coast or the Bay of Biscay. The expedition would break up into small parties racing in every direction, disrupting wireless and telegraphic communications as they went and giving the impression by the signals they sent out that they formed part of a large force travelling at great speed. They would destroy what they could as they went. As the Germans had little armour in France, some vehicles would reach their objectives and destroy them before any real opposition developed. Those who reached their destinations might or might not, according to their luck and successful planning, be picked up by submarines or fast craft. And they might, he added, stop long enough at Vichy to capture or hang most of the government as they raced through.

7

Many writers, including Sir Winston Churchill and General de Gaulle, have described the series of misfortunes and blunders which led to the arrival in West African waters of a powerful Vichy squadron, three large modern cruisers, the *Georges Leygues*, the *Gloire* and the *Montcalm*, together with three light cruisers,

Audacieux, *Fantasque*, and *Malin*, reported to be about the fastest and best armed for their size in the world.

When, on Friday the 13th September, 1940, we in the *Westernland* heard the announcement on the BBC that this squadron had escaped from the Mediterranean it caused us immense concern. Had the Vichy government heard of our plans, we asked ourselves, as they well might have done, and was this an attempt, with German connivance, or perhaps on German orders, to thwart them?

"Friday the 13th is always a day to beware of," said de Gaulle portentously. The most likely explanation that occurred to us was that Marshal Pétain had wished to make sure that no more French colonies rallied to de Gaulle and if possible to try to induce those who had done so to return to the fold.

Whatever Vichy had in mind and whatever the orders of the French admiral, the appearance of these ships in West African waters and the possibility that they might be making for Dakar could but present a grave threat to our expedition. It was obviously of vital importance that they should not sail farther south than Casablanca, or that if they did they should be invited to return there. It was also evident that it was highly unlikely that there were any British ships either in the North Atlantic or in the Mediterranean near enough in time or space to intercept them. I sent a signal, in agreement with General de Gaulle, to Admiral Cunningham in the *Devonshire* asking whether he would consider sending back part of his fleet to intercept the Vichy ships and compel them to return to Casablanca if they had sailed south of it.

His answer was that the provision of water in his ships was too low to allow him to do this.

I also asked whether he would send a cutter for General de Gaulle and me so that we might confer with him and General Irwin.[1]

He answered at 7 pm that he would see us as soon as we reached Freetown, but at 1 am a signal from the flagship announced that the admiral and General Irwin were coming over.

[1] General Irwin was GOC British troops. He and Admiral Cunningham were joint commanders of the Dakar expedition.

Such occasions at sea can be very dramatic.

As the *Westernland* came to a stop, wallowing in the slowly heaving sea which gurgled as it gently slapped the sides of our ship far down below the deck we stood on, we watched the lovely silvery road laid by the moon across the ink-blue sea. Then like a vast shadow silhouette drawn across it, appeared the great bulk of the *Devonshire*. A moment later, a dot could be perceived on the dazzling track, a little more permanent, slightly less ephemeral than the shadows that came and went by the thousand, marking with black stains the silver sheet spread before us. It was the cutter carrying the admiral and General Irwin. As it approached, and just before we started down to meet the visitors, I had occasion to thank my stars that my career had not been a naval one and that I had therefore never been a midshipman, for the unfortunate youth in charge of the cutter was told off for the mistakes he committed, imperceptible from the deck of the *Westernland*, in a series of roars and bellows that echoed and resounded over the South Atlantic rollers, making me feel that if the bold mariners from Toulon could have heard them they would have turned about and fled back to the Mediterranean in dismay.

Strangely enough, I remember well, and still think I could find my way along the endless companionways we hurried down in the dimmest of light into the bowels of our incredibly deep ship.

We missed the boarding party but were presently all assembled in the captain's cabin.

It was a relief to be together, to be actually able to speak to each other, to exchange ideas, instead of being isolated after the fashion of fish in different tanks in an aquarium. Together it would be easier to convey a picture to London.

It was a strange council of war, held in that dark and hideously hot and airless cabin, where the participants with shining, streaky, yellow faces clutched long glasses containing warm whisky, as they discussed the situation, the Englishmen at great pains to ensure that de Gaulle understood all that was said. A queer night, certainly a very queer night.

It was decided that with such ships as had the speed to do so, the admiral would make a determined attempt to compel any of the Vichy ships found south of Casablanca to return there.

In addition, my suggestion that d'Argenlieu should embark in a destroyer and personally order the Vichy ships to turn about was accepted. I thought they might find it easier to obey so humiliating an order if it was conveyed by a Frenchman, whilst not missing the point that it must be obeyed since it was given from the deck of a British warship.

On this occasion the fact that d'Argenlieu was a monk proved very useful, for a man of God has but few possessions. His preparations were the fastest I have ever seen. He was ready in well under ten minutes.

He did in fact catch up in a destroyer with two Vichy cruisers which had engine trouble. They meekly sailed for Casablanca at his order. But when this happened, the bulk of the Vichy fleet, unknown to us, were already at Dakar. Indeed, they were already there when we bade farewell to our visitors, who, in a few moments, became once again just one dark spot among many bespattering the heaving shimmering silver sea stretching before us like an immense scintillating scarf spread over the water.

Admiral Cunningham and General Irwin, both involved in the will o' the wisp pursuit of the French ships, were lost to us for a while, but they never for a moment ceased working, and inundating us with the results of their labours.

Their industry was in fact amazing. They later became my valued friends; but at the time I hardly knew them and wondered at the amount of paper they jointly produced, which reached us every few days in disconcertingly large bundles, plans to meet every emergency, excepting, as it turned out, the one with which we were presently faced.

When, having reached Freetown, we had the thrill of seeing the fleet steam by us, implacable as fate, stern as justice, unrelenting as doom yet as beautiful as swans slipping silently over the waves, we realised we had seen something never to be forgotten, an experience incredibly good for morale.

Freetown I found had little to commend it, but its approach from the magnificent estuary was very beautiful and reminiscent of Dublin Bay.

The shortage of small naval craft was something unbelievable. I think the only launch was that of the Admiral, South Atlantic, whose HQ Freetown was. So no one was allowed to land. Consequently eleven legionaires tried to swim ashore, and not one of them made it.

Freetown bay was a wonderful sight, with many ships dotted about its vast expanse protected only by what seemed to the uninitiated to be a very inadequate boom.

While we were in harbour awaiting our orders a most serious error became apparent. The ships had been stowed with but little regard to the operational plan as regards either weapons or material, with the result that material essential to a landing was found to be scattered among different ships and so stowed that there were neither the facilities nor the time to remedy the mistakes.

On the 17th September the *Devonshire*, having failed to intercept the Vichy squadron which by now was safe at Dakar, sailed into Freetown with Admiral Cunningham, General Irwin and Commandant d'Argenlieu on board. The latter had gathered from his contacts with the Vichy French that morale was low at Dakar. The first thing de Gaulle and I did was to inform the commanders that on the previous day the British government had sent a signal saying that in their view the arrival of the French cruisers had rendered the plan to gain control of Dakar impossible, and that we had both protested against this decision.

De Gaulle argued the advantages of consolidating the position acquired by the Free French, and the danger of delay, which would enable Vichy to counteract what had been achieved in rallying the Cameroons and French Equatorial Africa.

He begged that, even if the British government persisted in calling off the operation they had planned, they would at least concede air and naval support to an operation he meant to lead overland against Dakar.

De Gaulle and I were both glad to find that the commanders had reacted as we had and had sent signals to London on similar lines to ours. Meanwhile we awaited the government's decision. The very complicated question of fixing a date for the operation, should it be finally sanctioned, was discussed. It was no easy matter; the sea operations must obviously be synchronised with the pro-Free French rising inside the city which de Gaulle's representative, Captain de Boislambert, was organising. After his success in rallying the Cameroons, he had been summoned to join us at Freetown to be given his next task, to rally de Gaulle sympathisers in Dakar. He had to get some of his men into the place, but not too long ahead of the main operation. He and one or two more had to get into the city, some by native canoe from the Gambia, a most dangerous trip, and there was really no time to hope for reports from Dakar before the operation was launched, even supposing it would be possible to pass information back without alerting the authorities. Boislambert had asked that he should be given three days' warning of the attack, which proved in practice impossible. This aspect of the plan was evidently a considerable gamble, but basing himself on reports received and Boislambert's optimism and proved courage and determination, General de Gaulle placed very great hopes on its success.

There were some quite clear differences of opinion and sharp discussions during the numerous meetings on board either the *Devonshire* or the *Westernland* as to who should exercise command should a landing take place, as the orders issued to the commanders seemed to differ in spirit from what General de Gaulle had understood they would be, but in the end a solution was arrived at.

In these difficult talks and negotiations I found myself generally supporting General de Gaulle's point of view. This, however, did not apply to his claim to command all troops when landed "on French soil" including the British and Poles as well as his own. He may have misunderstood the agreements reached in London about this, though I hardly think so, for the Prime Minister had laid it down with some emphasis that if a mixed force were engaged the command must be British.

It was over this sort of question that de Gaulle was most difficult, and there were some sharp clashes, in particular with General
Irwin, before the question of command was finally settled in
conformity with the commanders' instructions.

It had by now been settled that, should the operation proceed,
Commandant d'Argenlieu, accompanied only by one or two
junior officers, should make for Dakar in a launch while the fleet
remained on the horizon. He was to go straight into the harbour
at the best speed his launch could command, land and ask to be
taken to the governor to whom he was to deliver an ultimatum
demanding that the Free French be allowed to land.

It was in the course of these discussions that I said I was quite
prepared to be landed at Dakar myself should Commandant
d'Argenlieu's mission fail. The idea did not appeal to me. I have
always feared above anything else being made a prisoner, and in
this case should things go wrong resistance would have been useless, but I felt bound to volunteer if there was the least chance of
my being useful. The advantages were, I thought, that whereas
the French might shoot at their compatriots they were unlikely
to do so at a solitary British general in uniform. If I went in alone
I would be able to explain what our objective was. This would
probably delay hostile action by the Dakar authorities, which
might prove to be important. When talking has started it is difficult to switch over to offensive measures. But there was the obvious disadvantage that this would give the whole action a British
character which would be most undesirable. The result might
well be to diminish de Gaulle's role, which was the opposite of
what was intended.

The final view of the commanders, which was accepted by us,
was that I should land if d'Argenlieu or the French authorities
asked for me but would not do so if d'Argenlieu's mission failed.

The result of these many anxious and concentrated discussions
was that during the night of the 17th September the admiral and
General Irwin finally concluded that the arrival of the three
Vichy cruisers at Dakar had not sufficiently increased the risk to
justify the abandonment of the expedition, and that the danger

of abandoning it presented the greater disadvantage. De Gaulle and his emissaries were convinced that the people and the soldiers, in fact all except the sailors, would rally to him. The way in which the Cameroons and Equatorial Africa had rallied was, after all, very encouraging and coloured the discussions at Freetown.

Late that night, after the Commanders had returned to their ship, they sent a signal to London saying that de Gaulle insisted upon the necessity of early action in Dakar and that they supported his view.

The plan agreed upon was a return to the original one, which consisted in an attempt by the Free French ships to sail into the harbour hoping for no opposition. Should this fail Free French troops would land nearby at Rufisque supported by naval and air action if necessary. British troops were only to be landed if called upon after the bridgehead had been established.

On the 18th I received a signal inviting me to inform General de Gaulle that his appeal to be allowed to proceed with the landing was receiving favourable consideration.

The next message gave the commanders full authority to do what they thought was best.

The prime minister was to write later that if those on the spot thought it was a time to do and dare the government would give them a free hand. He remarked, "It was very rare, at this stage of the war, for Commanders on the spot to press for audacious courses. Usually the pressure to run risks came from home."

I do not propose to describe the engagement of Dakar in detail. This has been done by others.

The operation was launched on the 23rd September in thick fog.

At 6 am the battleship *Barham*, now the flagship, reported that the two tiny Free French Luciole aeroplanes had landed successfully. It was intended that they should seize Ouakram aerodrome.

At 6 am the two launches carrying d'Argenlieu and the officers accompanying him were lowered from the Free French ship *Savorgnan de Brazza* three miles from the entrance to the harbour. The launches flew the Tricolour with the Cross of Lorraine and white flags of truce. D'Argenlieu landed at 7.30.

Meanwhile, as had been arranged, the British fleet closed in to a distance where, but for the fog, they could have been seen from the forts without running undue risk from the shore batteries.

De Gaulle and I had been standing long before dawn on the bridge of the *Westernland* peering into the dark dripping warm wetness of the tropical fog. We all believed that this was an unusually thick as well as a particularly unwelcome sea mist which was certain to be dispelled by the rising sun. We were shocked to learn later that fog was a common phenomenon on the coast at this time of year. It seems incredible that the naval authorities were not aware of this, for had they been they would surely have taken care to ensure that the operation was not started while there was any serious likelihood of fog.

It presently transpired that the Lucioles which had landed on Ouakram air strip, far from rallying the Vichy airmen as had been hoped, had been captured together with their crews.

As the light increased it was possible to see how restricted visibility was. Sounds were muffled as they always are by damp air.

One of General de Gaulle's signallers stood to one side of us. Why this obscure little sailor, holding his heavy shuttered lamp, his cap topped by its soaked pompon, now neither gay nor bright red, should have remained in my mind I cannot think, but he was more important than he seemed to be at the time, quietly awaiting orders in an operation the purpose of which he did not try to understand, probably rather uncertain on what sea the ship carrying him was swaying, content to obey as he always had been, whether to make a signal, haul up a sail or haul in a net on the Brittany coast before returning to the little harbour he told me of and which I remembered. It was perhaps because he represented confident, unquestioning discipline, because his look was so trusting and friendly, that he remains in my memory, as if through him I had extended a hand over a long period of time to the Breton fishermen of my childhood, obliterating the painful pictures of the French ratings at Aintree. A clumsy, inelegant little figure, but one I would be happy to have within hailing distance if I ever found myself engaged in another adventure at sea.

It has been the fate of all to wait and wait for news, with a sense of growing anxiety, but those who have had to undergo this ordeal in a fog, uncertain towards which point the ear should strain, know that its damp opacity is far worse than darkness.

At times the sky offered some deceptive visibility which induced a false impression of being able to see a little way, but we soon realised that this was a delusion, since only the sense of hearing warned us of a passing vessel.

At last some of our naval aircraft appeared, very slow and flying low towards Dakar. We knew they carried nothing more lethal than pamphlets announcing General de Gaulle's arrival, and when the French fired at them we realised the sort of reception the parliamentarians under d'Argenlieu, then on their way, were likely to receive.

Some of our planes were shot down in that shark infested sea. The orders were that no ship was to stop to pick anyone up, for it would have endangered its safety to do so. The fury I felt that our lads should face such a death on a peaceful mission was too deep ever to be forgotten.

At 9.15 am d'Argenlieu's launch appeared out of the mist. His mission had failed. An attempt had been made to arrest him and his party. They had jumped into their boat but were fired on. Both he and another officer accompanying him were wounded. D'Argenlieu's wound was painful but he remained cheerful, and I realised I had grown greatly to like this dapper little naval monk. Nothing at all encouraging had occurred so far, but we could and did hope that if the fog lifted we would see some sign that General de Gaulle's emissary, Captain de Boislambert, who it was hoped had got into Dakar, had not failed in his purpose of rallying the non-naval part of the population in favour of Free France.

We feared, however, that the Vichy ships must have brought a considerable number of Vichy militia, indoctrinated Fascist troops, to Dakar. These, we thought, might have succeeded in cowing the town, for we had been led to believe by Gaullist elements that, left to themselves, the population and the garrison would take the first opportunity to rally to de Gaulle. We heard later that shortly before we appeared before Dakar all the possibly friendly colonial gunners in charge of the coastal batteries had been replaced by naval gunners who were certainly hostile.

Meanwhile de Gaulle broadcast at intervals. I listened to some of his speeches, admirable in themselves, but wondered whether the sailors, enclosed and isolated in their ships, or the officials at their desks, even heard them, or if they did whether, under the eye and supervision of their chiefs, they could have responded to his call had they wanted to. Did any of the native population hear him and would they have realised what it was all about if they had?

It was becoming difficult to suppress the feeling that impetus was being lost, that the fog, like a slimy jelly-fish, was gradually enfolding us, depriving us of movement. But difficulties (if not these) and opposition had been foreseen, and all else failing we still hoped to land at Rufisque, from whence, provided the Free French detachments could be put ashore and be followed up promptly by reinforcements, Dakar could be occupied that night or next day.

Quite soon it became evident that communications, as if they too were becoming affected by the fog, were becoming clogged. The radio telephones went out of order, the wireless seized under the enormous pressure of messages, and visual signalling did not work for the obvious reason that we were all lost in invisibility. It then dawned on me that the navy was extraordinarily backward in the matter of communications and still apparently clung to the idea that a battle could be directed and controlled by a commander stationed half way up a mast on his flagship. I wondered by what lack of constructive imagination the Admiralty had failed to devise floating post offices provided with every conceivable signalling system to enable an admiral to communicate with and control his fleet many miles away.

The minutes slopped their damp way round the clock as we wallowed athwart the warm, glaucous, sticky rollers, engaged in a meaningless game of blind man's buff. A fish in strange waters where lurked rapacious enemies would have had a similar experience of helpless expectancy, for we only had the vaguest idea of what was afoot, what anybody was doing, where anybody was.

But the silence was alive with the suspected presence of ships great and small, until suddenly the air was torn by the discharge of great shells, causing air movements so violent as to shake one's head as if under the impact of a blow, generally followed by the incredibly harsh detonation of smaller guns firing in rapid succession, sledge hammer assaults on the eardrum. There were silences, if a sudden cessation of noise when the senses are tautly preparing for the next clamour can be termed a silence. Then, bewildered in spite of all anticipation, one would be thrown off one's guard, lassoed in a noose of trackless sound and jerked into goose-skinned apprehension.

The climax of noise occurred at 11.5 am when the British fleet opened fire in answer to that of the shore batteries and the *Richelieu*. The effect of this riposte, though we did not know it, was to set the Vichy warships moving about the harbour in the hope of avoiding being hit, but this was no easy manoeuvre, for fifty-four merchant ships were anchored there in addition to the naval craft.

It was about then that a Vichy submarine, the *Persée*, was sunk after launching torpedoes at a British cruiser.

The shelling in the fog was far worse than shelling at night, for its revolving opaqueness gave ghostly animation to what would otherwise have been a mere lack of light; it not only concealed the enemy as darkness would have done, it gave the impression of being a piece of sorcery evoked by him to wrap and conceal himself in.

As we stood on the drenched bridge, helpless, blind and uninformed, hope of success otherwise than by a landing which would take Dakar from the rear fell away minute by minute, as did the drops of water bedewing our coats.

Deprived of any sort of action, I remembered the battles I had known, and can well recall thinking that however little there was

to be said for land battles, which were singularly devoid of amenities, claustrophobia magnified the terrors of a sea engagement into something far worse. The sensation of being about as free of
one's movements, as unable to avoid danger as a sardine in its
box, was trying to one used to relying on movement for
safety.

The *Westernland* moved slowly or stopped, hoping for information and for instructions. News was received that the two Free
French sloops, the *Commandant Dominé* and the *Commandant
Duboc*, which had been ordered to enter the harbour and land
detachments, had been fired on and had turned back.

Our escorting destroyer had completely disappeared. The only
craft that made fitful and uncomfortably close appearances was
the food ship *Belgravia*, as dangerous and inopportune as would
have been an ox destined for the main course dashing in with the
hors d'oeuvres.

Communications were becoming ever more and more erratic,
Delphic and meaningless, bearing no relation to the question last
asked though they might have provided the answer to a query
put hours before concerning a situation which had perhaps never
materialised.

Only one thing was now clear: our forebodings that the operation had failed were confirmed, leaving open only the landing at
Rufisque. A message finally came through that this operation was
to be carried out. The heavy firing had long since ceased.

In a mist still limiting visibility severely but less thick and more
luminous, we moved and lolled our way towards land, following
the Free French ships, the *Duboc*, the *Dominé* and the *Savorgnan de
Brazza*.

Presently, at no great distance to our left, that is to the west, we
heard the clear rattle of musketry and the tut-tut of a machine-
gun, no great volume of fire, but it seemed evident that the landing was being attempted and was meeting with some opposition.
But from what we could hear this did not appear to be strong,
and we felt that a determined effort might well succeed. This
was encouraging, but it was disconcerting that there seemed to

be so little drive behind the attack. Very light musketry fire, only a few gunshots.

About then the admiral signalled that as he could not know the result of the action at Rufisque in time to develop his operation as planned he proposed to issue an ultimatum of one hour to the governor of Dakar, the landings to continue meanwhile. Did de Gaulle agree?

De Gaulle answered that he was suspending the landing at Rufisque by the men from the troopship (this had not started) because of the admiral's ultimatum, but was meanwhile landing the *fusiliers marins* from the sloops.

Half an hour later de Gaulle again signalled the admiral that the *fusiliers marins* were landing, and that he was awaiting news before deciding on landing the main body, whereupon two signals from the flagship came in at about the same time, the one asking, "Where are you?" and the other "Cancel Charles" (that is the landing of the main body of the Free French at Rufisque).

Our impression of what had occurred at Rufisque was correct, for natives had actually helped to haul up some of the Free French boats, and the opposition from a company of native troops had been of the lightest, apparently half-hearted and supported by most ineffective rifle fire. A few hits had been scored on the Free French sloops by a field battery, but not enough to have stopped troops with a minimum of training. But the Free French *fusiliers marins* had neither leadership nor training, not even the minimum required for brave men to dash for an objective. This led to their failure, not lack of courage. Some of them, we learned later, ran up the rough jetty abutting on the quay, but were driven back by some Negro soldiers urged to action by a white subaltern. It was pathetic.[1]

---

[1] The liaison officers under the British military commander reported that no landing had in fact taken place. It may well be that in the bad visibility they had not seen the small detachment that did land and was at once driven off.

The landing of the French was strictly de Gaulle's affair, and I do not recall his informing us of what his plan was, and all realised it was best not to enquire for fear of seeming to be inquisitive or revealing a tendency to interfere in a purely French affair.

The distant uncertain sounds from Rufisque had evoked a picture not very unlike what the reality turned out to be. It was maddening to stand idly by in this great ship as she swayed wallowing in the swell. Presently the captain, completely imperturbable, came along to say that we were closer inshore than was prudent, some two miles from Rufisque. One could not be quite certain of the depths given on the chart, and he could hear the waves breaking. He would, however, do whatever he was told. And I thought of the vast concourse of invisible men in that huge ship.

For some time I, and no doubt others, had observed an unmistakable Vichy plane, a Glen Martin, quartering backwards and forwards between our ship and Dakar at some two thousand feet, quite visible, for the fog had lifted at that height. With none to interfere it was evidently observing us with great ease and care. Then it disappeared as if intending to land for the pilot to make a personal report.

We were still wondering what the result would be when Major Watson, my personal assistant, appeared, calling out as he ran that two fast cruisers had broken out from Dakar.

De Gaulle knew as well as I did that if the cruisers opened fire on us, defenceless and undefended as we were, it would mean a holocaust. Our ship, packed with troops, would burn like a torch until it sank into that shark-infested sea. This was one of the very rare occasions when de Gaulle consulted me. "What do you think we should do?" He was pale and no doubt so was I. "There is absolutely no choice," I said. "We must turn away to sea as fast as we can, and the ship should turn outwards. From what the captain said the water is not deep enough to make an inward turn towards the coast possible. The captain should be told at

It is probable that de Gaulle's plan included either landing the troops from the ships' life-boats onto the beaches, which we had been told was generally possible at that time of year, or, more probably, disembarking at the jetties. But there had been no drill or practice of getting the men into the ship's boats. The only thing we knew had occurred was that volunteers from the ship's company had been asked for to man the life-boats and that all the British sailors had volunteered and all the Dutch had refused.

once," and we turned, but the breakers sounded very near as the great ship, like a horse pulled back on its haunches, seemed to halt in the act of suddenly changing its course. As the sound diminished, I think we both realised that the averted danger also meant hopes dying, drowned by the muted crash of the great Atlantic rollers.

I believe that experts, later following our course and that of the cruisers, were baffled by the fact that we and the Vichy cruisers did not run into each other.

De Gaulle and I did little talking. Once during the evening he said to me that he intended assuming the responsibility for having broken off the action. I told him that he had had no choice in the matter and that, as far as that went, I must share responsibility with him. No one but a lunatic could have taken any other decision. Once more, on this occasion as on others, General de Gaulle's attitude in adversity compelled admiration while rejecting sympathy.

Soon after we had turned our backs on Rufisque we were assigned a destination on the southern horizon towards which we steamed over a sea now clear of fog.

As we sailed on through the night, the suspense in our ship was very great. The fate of the expedition was being decided by others, elsewhere, in the flagship. It was clear that the attempt to seize Dakar having failed, the only thing left was the bombardment of the defences by the British fleet.

Would the commanders decide on the bombardment, and if so when?

Just after 11 pm, in answer to a signal from de Gaulle asking the commanders for their appreciation of the situation, they answered that they felt that the reduction of the forts and the destruction of the ships would lead to the collapse of resistance. Consequently, they added, if their ultimatum was not accepted by 6 am on the 24th, they intended to proceed with the systematic destruction of the defences, later landing troops as required. The end of the signal was corrupt but indicated that the Prime Minister had sent a message, which, both according to what was comprehensible in the text and from the obvious deduction to be drawn from the Commanders' message, encouraged them to carry on with the operation. What Churchill had in fact signalled was: "Having begun we must go on to the end. Stop at nothing."

In answer to this signal, General de Gaulle repeated an earlier request that the admiral should make it clear to the Dakar authorities that the Free French forces were not now involved, and that he had withdrawn them.

Next morning, the 24th, heavy gunfire many miles to the north of where we and the other transports were cruising gave a clear indication that the bombardment was on, but we had no indication of the degree or strength of the Vichy response. It seemed evident, however, to the distant observers we were, that there was little ground for optimism, for had the defence collapsed our bombardment would have ceased instantly and we would no longer hear rumbling, punctuated by irregular bursts of louder noises the violence of which distance could not entirely muffle.

At about 10 am the bombardment ended, but we had no idea what this portended. It was resumed again for a short time in the early afternoon.

It must have been about 3 pm, as de Gaulle and I were attempting to draw up an appreciation of the situation, when without any warning, in complete silence, out of nowhere, the fleet appeared. It was extraordinarily dramatic and had some of the elements of a miracle. At one moment nothing but an expanse of short choppy deep blue waves chasing each other in bad-tempered dishevelled games of tip and run, then the sea was covered as far as the eye could see with an archipelago of ships.

As I was watching these ships, deeply moved by the feeling that they were the very embodiment of what Britain stands for, a small aircraft came in sight, flying towards the *Barham* like a tired homing pigeon making a great effort to reach its loft, then it dived and disappeared into the sea. It was the sort of sight that squeezes the heart in anguish. We heard afterwards that the young pilot had been saved, but I have not forgotten the horror of watching through glasses his sun helmet appear intermittently on the waves.

Then a destroyer appeared, rolling and pitching in the heavy sea. It lowered a whaler which was to convey General de Gaulle and me to the *Barham*, to which the admiral had transferred his flag.

I shall always remember the long pull in that whaler. Like every other Englishman I have what might be described as a religious veneration for the image the navy conjures up in the mind of every one of us, but never have I admired it so much as that afternoon. The destroyer to which the men at the oars belonged had suffered some casualties from one or more shells that had gone right through it. They had had no sleep and were worn out. I do not think I had ever before seen sailors anything but spick and span. These looked like very tired pirates rescued from a battle-worn ship. The lesson they conveyed was of calm fortitude, of unruffled courage. Nor could I forget the wonderful petty officer in charge. He has his place among the few men to whom in the course of my life I have paid a silent tribute of admiration for outstanding qualities of leadership. Very gently, yet resolutely and firmly, he urged his weary crew on to make the necessary rhythmic effort to drive the boat forward.

Getting on board the *Barham* was not at all easy. The swell seemed to be running counter to the wind, and we appeared to sink to great depths, then without warning to be thrown very high. There was a projection, a bulge on the ship's side under which we seemed to have a tendency to slip; had we been caught under it we would have been pushed under water with a violent blow comparable to that with which a champagne cork is driven home at bottling.

On board, the men were in the nondescript clothing they had worn during the action. They looked odd and unshaven and very tired, but behind their reserve and the perceptible veil of discipline they showed friendliness towards these land soldiers, the French and the English, thrown up by the blue ridged sea that tropical afternoon. Their curiosity was almost palpable. What did our visit portend?

Had they known, they would not have been greatly cheered, for nothing very clear emerged. The commanders wanted to know General de Gaulle's views before taking their own decision, which would of necessity also be influenced by possible further instructions from London, news of Vichy reaction, visibility and weather conditions, and reports concerning the effect of the operation on the garrison and population. The meeting was in reality a twilight council, the inquest on an operation that had failed. It had some of the elements of an old Irish wake at which the participants try to pretend the corpse is not dead.

The meeting, which took place on the admiral's bridge, never fell below the highest level of mutual courtesies. There were no recriminations, no scapegoats were sought. Concerning the fog only were strong opinions expressed. General de Gaulle showed at once that his mood was on no less high a plane than that of the British commanders: he was emphatic in wishing to assume responsibility for having withdrawn from the action outside Rufisque. All the Englishmen present appreciated the high-minded generosity of this man who had lost so many hopes in the Dakar fog but was anxious nevertheless to claim his full share, and more than his share, of responsibility for the failure. De Gaulle saw clearly what was essential to him: the world must be told and told again that Dakar had opened fire first; that it was he, de Gaulle, who had ordered the withdrawal of the landing party to avoid fighting between Frenchmen. That this was something of an euphemism, as was his subsequent statement that the Free French at Rufisque were unarmed, was little more than an instance of the stresses wartime propaganda is subject to.

De Gaulle was very anxious that it should be made clear that he had no responsibility for any action the commanders might take from now on. He only requested that the Vichy ships should not be allowed to sail south.

The admiral gave us a summary of what had happened during the action.

On the 23rd, when the shore batteries had opened fire on the fleet, the *Cumberland* had been hit and had had to retire. Two destroyers, one of them the *Inglefield* which had provided the whaler that had just brought us to the flagship, had been slightly damaged. We learnt without surprise that the fog had been a "damned nuisance", but if it had hindered our ships it must have been a handicap to the Vichy shore batteries also, whose fire had nevertheless proved to be remarkably accurate.

Careful examination of the facts established that the Vichy guns had opened fire first.

On the morning of the 24th, when the bombardment by the fleet began, visibility had been much better than on the previous day, but still poor. The *Barham* and the *Resolution* had engaged the *Richelieu* at 13,600 yards and it was thought she had been hit by a 15″ shell (this proved not to be true). The Vichy losses were believed to amount to a destroyer hit and a submarine which had been forced to the surface and had surrendered. None of the British ships were hit. When the bombardment had been resumed for a short time in the afternoon the *Barham* had been hit four times but, as we could see for ourselves, no serious damage had been done. Our naval aircraft had made several attacks in the course of which a number were lost, without apparently achieving any result.

It was evident that the guns of the *Richelieu* had tended to reduce the advantage of the British fleet in gun power and to re-establish the superiority, recognised by Nelson, of shore batteries over guns mounted on ships; its 15″ guns had deprived the fleet of the possibility of pounding the shore batteries whilst remaining out of gunshot, as the range of the *Richelieu's* guns matched those of the heaviest British armament.

The commanders gave us the impression that at the moment at least they were not in favour of renewing the attack. Observation from the air, owing to the aggressiveness of the Dakar planes, was not easy, and smoke screens had made accurate shooting difficult. General Irwin thought that now that it had been proved that it was difficult to ensure that the Vichy ships did not leave the harbour, an attempt to land troops would be a very hazardous enterprise, and de Gaulle thought so too. We were told that the governor of Dakar had answered the last ultimatum by saying he would defend the fortress to the last.

When de Gaulle was asked what in his opinion the effect of the bombardment was likely to have been on the population of Dakar, he answered that he thought it would certainly have antagonised them.

What made the prospect of any further action even less encouraging than a plain assessment of the meagre results achieved, was the information that more Vichy warships including the *Strasbourg* were reported to have left Toulon and that it was possible that Vichy aircraft and reinforcements might well be on their way to Dakar. That Gibraltar had been heavily bombed by Vichy planes was a clear indication of the Pétain Government's reaction.

General de Gaulle said that he would like to land his troops at Bathurst in the Gambia to exercise them and glean whilst there what news he could of what was going on in French West Africa. He asked that a signal be sent to the Governor asking if he had any news of de Gaulle's emissary to Dakar, Captain de Boislambert, and his companions. There was none, nor was there any indication of a pro-de Gaulle movement in Dakar.

During the whole of this gloomy exchange of views, from which no light emerged, I had been watching the admiral, whose attention was focused with growing strain and anxiety on the wooden gratings of the bridge, into the deep cavities of which General de Gaulle, who never ceased smoking, kept throwing a constant stream of burning cigarette ends. Down they came like incadescent meteorites with an appropriate escort of match ends. No battleship deck, at least in the British navy, can ever have been treated with such contumely, and the outraged admiral, forgetting Dakar for a moment, propelled an empty pompom shell case towards de Gaulle for him to use as an ashtray. The Frenchman, hardly perceiving it, yet conscious of it as might a sportsman on the edge of a wood awaiting pheasants be aware of the flight of a jay, threw a cigarette end in its direction and missed. Whereupon another shell case was pushed towards him until he was surrounded by them as if he himself had been a pompom firing in a heavy engagement, while the distracted admiral watched the cigarette ends in flight with the hypnotised attention of a Wimbledon fan following a champion's service.

I have a vague recollection that our departure from the battleship to return to the *Westernland* involved some startling movements by our whaler, during which our preoccupation was not to appear too clumsy, too awkward before the sailors. Apart from that there was nothing but the morose roughness of the implacably blue sea. There are occasions when nothing can be more depressing than a cloudless sky and harsh shadows. Back on board, we found our little sailor monk, d'Argenlieu, chirpy and cheerful though still in considerable pain in his suffocating cabin.

Early on the morning of the 25th September a signal was received from the commanders which indicated that, on fresh information, they had altered the point of view they had expressed at the conference in the *Barham*. In coming to their decision they probably had the Prime Minister's signal, that they were to stop at nothing, very much in mind. They said that air reports indicated that the damage to the Vichy cruisers and other naval vessels as well as to the land forts might have been more extensive than was at first thought, and that at least one more effort to test the defences should be made if the weather conditions were favourable.

As the hours passed, we in the *Westernland* did not know whether the action had in fact been resumed, though this might be inferred from the sound of distant gunfire, nor did we receive any explanation as to why our ship and the other transports had been ordered to sail southwards. We had only been told by the commanders that they had asked the government to adopt de Gaulle's proposal of the 24th to land his troops at Bathurst with a view to planning a land attack on Dakar. So, at 12.36 pm, we sent a signal to the admiral saying we knew nothing and asking why we were sailing southwards.

Optimistically, although very much in the dark, General de Gaulle and I signalled that, after a careful review of the land forces at his disposal, we thought that the Dakar operation in some form should not be abandoned.

We did not know that soon after 1 pm the Prime Minister had sent a signal stating that, unless something had happened the government did not know of which made the commanders wish to attempt a landing in force, the engagement should be broken off forthwith. This signal also said that, assuming the enterprise to be abandoned, British naval forces would endeavour to cover Douala but could not safeguard de Gaulle's forces in Bathurst.

The *Westernland* was back at Freetown at 8 am on the 27th. There we were told that the *Barham* was towing the *Resolution* at three or four knots to the south. She had been hit by a Vichy submarine at 9 am on the 25th. Later I saw the great battleship moving slowly with a heavy list. To the unprofessional she looked as if she might easily keel over in a heavy sea.

I have seen brave men, the pride of their unit, being led wounded off a battlefield. This was far more painful, for this helpless giant was one of England's hopes, and its plight was more shattering than any human loss could have been.

This tragic sight was for me my most heart-breaking experience of the whole Dakar engagement. In contrast to this tragedy, some of the actions of the Free French struck a note of macabre comedy: for instance the meeting between some of their officers and the Vichy naval prisoners. Both groups hated each other with a bitter hatred, yet having been at the Naval School, the *Bordat*, together could not help using the familiar '*tu*' to each other. They reviled each other intimately.

I also remember as strange and sad the enthusiasm with which the Free French sloops, which had an anti-aircraft armament infinitely superior to anything we possessed, fired at the Vichy planes flying over Freetown, putting to shame our amateur efforts. There was no hate here, it was just a matter of sport, the excitement of good shooting. This is a phenomenon I have observed in war. The man you are shooting at is just a target. You do not see him as a man who will suffer if hit, who may leave an irreparable gap if killed.

One of their targets was a Vichy Glen Martin aircraft which flew daily, leisurely, yet thorough reconnaissance flights over the great estuary from the shores of French Guinea opposite. Its reports on the assembled shipping it observed no doubt reached the Germans in no time. After much cogitation, the British colonial authorities decided that their totally inadequate anti-aircraft defences should also be allowed to fire at the visitor. When I saw the result I for one regretted having advocated this bellicosity, for all that happened was that some ten minutes after the plane had passed a few blobs of smoke appeared, daubing the sky with ugly grey puffs which might have been aimed at the sun, the moon, or indeed just into the blue sky for the sake of making a bang, so little connection did they have with the track of the vanished aircraft. But the acme of absurdity was reached when the legal authority of the colony declared, so we were informed, that these harmless puffs were quite illegal and that the only proper step open to us was to fine the intruder £100 every time he flew over the fleet!

Later I reported the story to Lord Lloyd, our very active Colonial Secretary, who quite failed to be amused by it. It was one of the reasons why, I believe, he made plans for a tour of the colonies which unfortunately did not take place owing to his death.

This attitude towards Vichy was typical of the vacillating military policy of our officials in West Africa. It was all so cosy and worked so nicely provided no one did anything to throw off balance the pleasantly adjusted relationship between neighbouring Vichy and British colonies. Africans, and especially French African soldiers, in considerable numbers, who tried to come over to enlist in de Gaulle's forces were severely discouraged as this would, and indeed did, annoy Vichy officials.

It was a matter of deep regret to me that the British military were more disposed to appease the Vichy authorities than was the Royal Navy. The former were subject to a kind of fluttering irresolution. The naval officers, on the other hand, seemed better conditioned to take quick clear decisions.

8

The events that followed the failure at Dakar are part of the history of the war.

It was only gradually that we realised that world opinion had judged the operation to be a major disaster. It was certainly a very serious setback, due to lack of knowledge of local conditions, which in turn led to the whole plan being built on false assumptions. Some things are difficult to excuse, for instance the ignorance of local weather conditions, and the faulty stowing of cargo, which made a change of plan, such as the landing of different troops to those at first detailed, impossible. Other mistakes were due to errors that constantly recur in human history, as for instance reliance on unchecked intelligence, on the belief that a population inclined to a cause will be prepared to risk inconvenience, let alone getting hurt, in the furtherance of its objective. In fact the risk it is hoped a well-disposed populace will run in support of the side it favours can only be reckoned and measured by the stake they hope to collect. If the fear inspired by the opponent is great and if he is ruthless and cruel you can expect little assistance from the spectators even if they hope for your success, and it is very rare that a rising will take place unless the ground has been carefully prepared. The population of Dakar and perhaps many of the garrison were inclined to de Gaulle's cause, but to risk prison and court martial for it was another matter.

A further mistake was to base a serious military operation on unverified and unverifiable political assumptions. The only political assumption it is ever safe to make is that all the doubtful factors will operate against you until you have clearly established your superiority, or give the impression of having done so.

I bear my own share of responsibility for what happened, having backed de Gaulle and the commanders wholeheartedly in their desire to persist in the operation in spite of the arrival of the Vichy reinforcements. The decision to cancel the Free French landing was inevitable in the circumstances, but I still believe that but for the chaotic conditions caused by the fog, the landing could have succeeded under the protection of the Free French ships and of the two British destroyers which were to have supported it but never appeared. Had the Foreign Legion and other French troops landed and called for support, as it was expected they would do, then the British and Polish troops would have landed, and I am confident that in that event Dakar would have fallen.

After Dakar the paths of the responsible leaders diverged. That of de Gaulle appeared to stretch, arid and ill defined, in no particular direction. I watched his lonely figure stalk off down it, and I can only be sure of one thing: that as he observed its steepness and the number of boulders that strewed it, the motive that impelled him on was not personal ambition. I am certain when he started the Free French movement it did not occur to him that one day he would lead his nation. He was convinced only that he must be prepared to undertake any task, face any difficulty and danger, for the sake of France. If no one else would lead then he would. If no one else would defy the Pétain government that had accepted surrender and national extinction, then he would do so, and would continue to proclaim that France was not dead if it cost him his last breath.

He had suffered one more set-back at Dakar, but it did not deter him. His duty was to attempt to free France. New obstacles might obstruct the road that lay ahead, but they would not stop him. His temperament dictated his outlook. He must walk alone. The stones he encountered he picked up and added to the burden he already carried, and it was the intolerable strain of constantly recurring rebuffs and disappointments that were, in part at least, responsible for his unfair and unjust suspicions, his vindictiveness and outbursts of ugly temper.

Englishmen, observing his remote and aloof bearing towards his own subordinates, concluded he was churlish by disposition. Few of them were familiar with the distant manner adopted by military seniors towards their juniors in the French army, something unknown in the British services, where juniors lived in familiar contact in their messes with their seniors, who were protected from familiarity by the good manners of commissioned officers drawn on the whole from social strata which imposed a common standard. In the French army the opening of commissioned rank to a much wider social field after the Revolution led to severe and clear-cut distinctions being drawn between the ranks. It is also true that de Gaulle adopted, as his position evolved and his responsibilities increased, the manner which his knowledge of French history led him to believe corresponded with the rank he had assumed. In later years this has induced some mocking ridicule, but none can deny that he has always maintained the dignity of the position he occupied.

I do not doubt that de Gaulle was convinced that France must either be a great nation or nothing more than a heap of shards, the glistening débris of what had once been one of the world's most beautiful ornaments, and my reason for thinking so was that even I, a foreigner, believed this to be true. For France is more than a thing of wit and beauty, she is a cornerstone of civilisation as we understand it; a crumbling sandstone in her place would threaten Europe's stability.

In rebuilding his country General de Gaulle has rendered the world a great service; it is unfortunate that the methods he employed for achieving this most desirable result have caused so much offence.

He realised two things were necessary to re-establish France, the first and by far the most important was to restore the confidence of the French in themselves and to build an honourable present worthy of her glorious past.

That past is illuminated by military victories, and such defeats as Waterloo are accepted as only the tragic end of a great epic, a long tale of endless triumphs.

This is not the British way. We, too, have won many battles, but only have a deep feeling about one of them, and that is a naval one. To us Waterloo is only a station, but Trafalgar is more than a square. We have always been more inclined to celebrate our defeats, from Hastings to Dunkirk, than our victories.

To the French people, the fearful defeat of the last war means much more than the suffering of enemy occupation, it represents a moral humiliation which lesser nations which suffered the same hardship never endured. General de Gaulle set himself the task of curing this moral hurt, of assuaging the haemorrhage of this mental wound. His methods seemed rough to onlookers, but were effective and appropriate to the mentality of his countrymen, which is very different from that of the British. De Gaulle's second objective, which was also necessary to successfully achieving the first, was to be strong or to appear to be strong, which is the same thing, for you are strong until others find you are not, and de Gaulle's superb and quite unique achievement has been to create an impression of strength out of helplessness until he was in fact powerful.

In French history and legend her often shattering defeats have been so presented to the people as to convince them that they were no fault of the nation.

The Franco-Prussian war of 1870–71 is a case in point.

Before 1940 other Frenchmen than de Gaulle had felt convinced that temporary adversity could not be held for a moment to mean that France was not unquestionably the leading nation of the world. When General Masséna, afterwards one of Napoleon's marshals, was forced to capitulate at Genoa in 1800, Lord Keith, the British admiral, as the conference laying down the surrender terms ended, in the rather sentimental melodramatic way which on occasion seems to seize Englishmen when dealing with the French, grasped Masséna's hand and exclaimed, "If only France and England could get together they could rule the world!" "*La France suffit,*" answered Masséna. As General Sir James Marshall-Cornwall in his excellent book, *Marshall Masséna* put it, "Charles de Gaulle could not have said it better".

Because he was a Frenchman de Gaulle understood the importance of *panache* to his countrymen, as necessary to them as is salt on an Englishman's plate.

There is no English word to translate what *panache* means to a Frenchman.

The average Englishman with a good knowledge of French would say it meant bravado, swagger. A Frenchman, asked the same question, would explain the idea by saying that Rostand's plays, *Cyrano de Bergerac* and *Chantecler* are the very essence of *panache*. Indeed is not the cock Chanticler the emblem chosen by the French themselves to represent France?

There is no French heart that is not uplifted when Cyrano, fighting to the last, declaims:

"*Samedi, vingt-six, une heure avant diner, Monsieur de Bergerac est mort assasiné.*"

Panache is an excellent word to express an attitude which appeals to the French and is redolent of victory, for it was probably born on a battlefield, when Henry IV, king of France, contemporary of our Queen Elizabeth and survivor of St Bartholomew's massacre, clad in his armour and about to lead a cavalry charge, pointed to the white plumes on his helmet and cried:

"Rally on my white plume" – "*Ralliez vous à mon panache blanc*". This, in the eyes of most Frenchmen, is the quintessence of *panache*.

Frenchmen themselves sometimes differ as to the application of the word: some think that Napoleon I was a master of the use of the conception of *panache* as for instance when, addressing the army in Egypt under the Pyramids he declared, "Forty centuries are watching you from the pinnacle of these pyramids", or later when, before a battle on a fine day, he exclaimed, "The Sun of Austerlitz is shining". But others will maintain that this was mere oratory by a master of theatrical effects, well calculated to raise morale but no more.

I have given earlier, a superb example of *panache* in the action of the mortally wounded French officer who, at the beginning of the battle of the Marne, seeing the Germans advancing once more, called to the wounded and dying men who surrounded him to stand up and fight on. "*Debout les morts!*" – "Up the dead!" he cried. And rise they did.

Some French people maintain that the acme of *panache* was the action of the St Cyr cadets, the equivalent of our Sandhurst, who when war was declared in 1914 took a collective oath to lead the red-trousered infantry of France into battle wearing the St Cyriens' beplumed headdress, the 'Casoar', and kid gloves. They kept their word and were mowed down in the great French offensives in August 1914. Such bravery, in British eyes, is as touching as it is foolish. It meant the sacrifice of a whole 'promotion' of St Cyr, the best of France's youth, which she could ill afford.

The English equivalent of *panache* is its exact opposite – understatement, on which we pride ourselves.

A classic example of this is the letter written by a naval officer, Captain Walton, of HMS *Canterbury*, to Admiral Byng after the battle of Passero in 1718.

Taken
One Spanish rear-admiral of
   60 guns
One man of war of 54
One of 40
One of 24
One ship laden with arms
One bomb vessel

Burnt
One man of war of 54
Two of 40 each
One of 30
One fireship
One bomb vessel
One settee

Sir,

   We have taken and destroyed all the Spanish ships and vessels which were upon the coast, the number as per margin.

      I am, etc.,

      G. WALTON

Searching for the form of *panache* General de Gaulle has found to take the place of Henry IV's plume or Cyrano's rhymes, I was lucky enough to put the question to a very wise Frenchman who gave me the instant reply:

"The *panache* that has rallied France is that having suffered humiliation and defeat and been treated as an insignificant power that

could never rise again, de Gaulle, in the name of all his countrymen, has challenged the most powerful nation in the world and
told America and the Americans to go to hell."

Which is not exactly what my friend said. He used the word the
commander of the Imperial Guard used when asked to surrender
at Waterloo, "*le mot de Cambronne*", which has been euphemis-
tically translated as "The Guard dies but never surrenders".

After the Dakar disaster I followed General de Gaulle's activities for some time, watching him consolidate in the face of great
difficulties the French West African colonies that had rallied to
him. He received little backing from the majority of French
settlers who, with some honourable exceptions, were only with
him because trade with neighbouring British possessions was
essential to them.

By 1941 I had founded the branch of my mission in Cairo
which presently formed the nucleus of the main mission in the
Levant, that is in Syria and the Lebanon.

In spite of some major differences due to de Gaulle's fundamental distrust of the British and their motives, he and I worked
in the closest accord to persuade the British government and
the military authorities to prevent the Vichy French from allowing the Germans to establish bases in the Levant. This led to the
Syrian campaign, as a result of which I remained in the Levant.
Thereafter I became first minister to Syria and the Lebanon, and
de Gaulle and I finally parted company over his attitude towards
the Levant states, whose independence we had guaranteed. But
that is another story.

It was the crucible of 1940 that transformed the obscure colonel
of the battle of France, whose only previous achievement had been
success in a minor tank battle. He emerged from it with his qualities of courage and self-reliance, audacity and daring, but also
with his defects of ingratitude, vindictiveness, duplicity and pre-
judice; all inherent in the metal, but turned into steel by the ordeals of that terrible summer.

In 1940 he proclaimed himself Joan of Arc. It was not long after the Dakar fiasco that he told the British Foreign Secretary, "*Je suis la France*".

He never, either then or later, hesitated to go banco, to stake his all on every throw of the dice.

He did not need to learn from Churchill a creed we sometimes seem to have forgotten but would do well to remember: boundless love of country and complete faith in its destiny. Whilst we have twice in thirty years won a war and lost a peace, de Gaulle, absolutely alone, has rebuilt his shattered country on the ruins of defeat, and has made France stronger, and her influence greater, than it has been for a century.

The man he is today, General de Gaulle, President of the Fifth Republic, was formed by the refractory processes to which he was subjected in those summer months twenty-five years ago.

Index

de Gaulle, (cont).

poses to establish a French National Defence Committee, 138–9; lack of response to his call for support, 140; condemned to death by Pétain and Weygand, 140, 149; British attitude to, and lack of understanding of, 141, 150, 159, 212; his distrust of Britain, 144–5, 149, 151, 158, 168; character and appearance, 144, 146–7, 149–50, 151–2; Churchill signs agreement to restore France's freedom, 145; his anxiety about his family's escape from France, 146; "I really am Joan of Arc", 147–8, 217; his rudeness – and courtesy, 148–9; his tribute to Britain's local invasion precautions, 150–1; visits camps of French troops in Britain, 152–3, 158–9; Churchill grants him permission to recruit Frenchmen in Britain, 152, 156–7; and the Cameroons, 152; British Government's ruling on the death penalty for Allied troops in England, 154; and consul's threats to troops wishing to join Free French, 155; and dilemma of the French Fleet at Oran, 160 ff.; castigates British press, 165; efforts to recruit support in French West African colonies, 174 ff.; attempts and failure to capture Dakar, 181 ff.; his understanding of Frenchmen's regard for panache, 214–15; as sole rebuilder of French power and influence ("I am France"), 218

Gaulle, Mme Charles de, 146
Gausse, Gen. (German army), 166
Gensoul, Admiral Marcel-Bruno, 161–4 passim, 167
Giffard, Gen. (general commanding British Forces in West Africa), 178, 179–80
Gort, Lord, 136
Gouraud, Gen., 63–4
Gwydyr House, Whitehall, 141

Haig, Gen. Sir Douglas, 24, 25, 27
Halifax, Lord, 134
Hankey, Col. (secretary to the cabinet), 43, 47
Holland, Capt. (one-time Naval Attaché in Paris), 164
Hopkinson, Henry (later Lord Colyton), 142

Indo-China, 139, 160
Irwin, Gen. (GOC British troops, West Africa), 183, 188–94 passim, 206
Ismay, Gen. Lord (Chief of Staff to Sir Winston Churchill), 140, 173

Joffre, Gen. Joseph, 12, 84, 182
Juba, 184

Keith, Lord (1st Viscount), 214
Koenig, Capt. (Foreign Legion), 153

Laffaux, 90
Lageay, Capt. Piet (commander of the Westernland), 185
Lagos, 177, 178
Larminat, Col. de, 176–7, 180
Laval, Pierre, 139
Le Gentilhomme, Gen. Paul, 139
Lebanon, the, 217
Leclerc de Hauteclocque, Commandant Philippe, 177–80 passim
Lewis, Col. Leroy (British military attaché), 35–6
Limoges, 41, 97
Liverpool, 167–71, 182
Lloyd, Lord, 152, 175, 210
Lloyd George, David, 20, 43–7
Lyons, 35

Malmaison, 25, 126
Malvy, Louis Jean (Minister of the Interior), 19, 28, 120, 127 n
Mandel, Georges, 136–7
Mangin, Gen., 51
Marshall-Cornwall, Gen. Sir James, 214